「平和宣言」を英語で読む

―ヒロシマの心

帝京大学出版会 編

Hiroshima
Peace
Declaration

JN104402

帝京新書
001

Contents

Chairman's Foreword

In 1966, Shinzo Hamai, then mayor of Hiroshima City, delivered a Peace Declaration at a ceremony to mark the 21st anniversary of the atomic bombing of the city.

Referring to the risk of an outbreak of nuclear war, Hamai stated, "We firmly believe that all nations and peoples should rise to the cause of human survival, laying aside all self-interests and past grievances, now that man has come to share his lot not so much with a particular nation as with the earth in its entity."

How well his Peace Declaration resonates with the United Nations Sustainable Development Goals (SDGs)! The foresight of the Peace Declaration, which warns of human extinction, is astonishing. I believe this is deeply related to the fact that he was an atomic bomb survivor.

Teikyo University was also founded in 1966.

In 2023, Teikyo University Press was established as part of the university's 60th anniversary commemorative project, and the "*Teikyo Shinsho*" series of books was launched in conjunction with the establishment of the Press. This is the first volume of the commemorative series.

Teikyo University, which initially opened with two faculties — the Faculty of Letters and the Faculty of Economics — now has 10 faculties and 11 graduate schools. We place great importance on "practical learning," as exemplified by the School of Medicine and the School of Pharmacy. The School of Medicine aims to foster good doctors.

A good doctor respects human life, whereas wars are waged with total disregard for human life. Nuclear weapons are the greatest threat to our survival.

For human life to be fully respected, there must be peace. Peace is the condition for human existence.

The Declaration of Peace, the Constitution of Japan, and the Charter of the United Nations are all guided by the principle of pacifism. These are the expression of our conscience that respects human life. They are also related to academic freedom and institutional autonomy that universities have cultivated since the Middle Ages in Europe.

This year marks the 80th anniversary of the "mobilization of students" in 1943. During World War II, the Japanese government sent university students to the battlefields to compensate for the shortage of troops due to the worsening military situation. Some students died in suicide attacks, while others died of war-related illnesses as well as starvation. If the students who were 20 years old at the time were still alive and well, they would be 100 years old today.

We have learned that university students must never be sent into battle again. No one should be allowed to deprive them of the opportunity to learn and study. War and nuclear weapons will never be compatible with universities.

We sincerely hope that you will read this book and think together with us about the preciousness of life, the blessings of peace, the stupidity of war, and the cruelty and inhumanity of nuclear weapons.

OKINAGA Yoshihito
Chairman
Teikyo University

PREFACE

In lieu of a preface, the following is the City of Hiroshima's explanation of the Peace Declaration:

In 1947, two years after Hiroshima experienced the tragedy of the world's first atomic bombing, the City of Hiroshima held a Peace Festival, in the hope that the Festival would develop into an event on a global scale and that it would help to convey Hiroshima's desire for lasting peace to the people of the world.

The three-day Festival started on August 5th, 1947. On August 6th, a ceremony was held in the area that was to eventually become the Peace Memorial Park. The first Peace Declaration was read by then-mayor Shinzo Hamai:

"This horrible weapon brought about a "Revolution of Thought," which has convinced us of the necessity and the value of lasting peace. That is to say, because of this atomic bomb, the people of the world have become aware that a global war in which atomic energy would be used would lead to the end of our civilization and extinction of mankind. This revolution in thinking ought to be the basis for an absolute peace, and imply the birth of new life and a new world...What we have to do at this moment is to strive with all our might towards peace, becoming forerunners of a new civilization. Let us join to sweep away from this earth the horror of war, and to build a true peace...Here, under this peace tower, we thus make a declaration of peace."

All of the cries against war and all of the genuine searching for peace welling up[1] from deep in the hearts of the people of Hiroshima took form in this document, the Peace Declaration.

The Peace Declaration has since been delivered by the mayor of Hiroshima every year at the August 6 Peace Memorial Ceremony, but its content has changed with the times. The words "against atomic and hydrogen bombs," first appeared in then-mayor Tadao Watanabe's 1956 Peace Declaration, a year after the first World Conference Against A -and H-Bombs. In 1971, 26 years after the end of World War II, then-mayor Setsuo Yamada used his Peace Declaration to make clear that peace education was necessary in order to hand down the meaning of war and peace to the next generation. In 1982, then-mayor Takeshi Araki incorporated into[2] his Peace Declaration a call to the cities of the world to answer the proposal for peace solidarity that was made at the Second UN Special Session for Disarmament[3] in June of that year. The solidarity of cities has spread to include many cities from all over the world as Mayors for Peace.

In the 1991 Peace Declaration, given the year he took office, then-mayor Takashi Hiraoka, a first for

---

1) welling up 湧き上がること、盛り上がること 2) be incorporated into~ ～に組み込まれる 3) Second UN Special Session for Disarmament 第二回国連軍縮特別総会

a mayor of Hiroshima, stated that, "Japan inflicted great suffering and despair on the peoples of Asia and the Pacific during its reign of colonial domination and war. There can be no excuse for these actions." In his 1996 Peace Declaration he stated his hope that agreement on the Comprehensive Nuclear Test Ban Treaty would lead to a total ban on nuclear tests, and called for the creation of a culture of peace and an archive of A-bombed materials to convey to as many as possible the reality of the atomic bombing. To realize a world without nuclear weapons, the 1997 Peace Declaration called upon "the government of Japan to devise security arrangements that do not rely on a nuclear umbrella." At the same time, it emphasized the necessity of candid dialogue amongst the people of the world to transcend[4] differences in language, religion and custom.

After taking office in 1999, then-mayor Tadatoshi Akiba commended the *hibakusha* (atomic bomb victims) in that year's Peace Declaration for transcending the suffering and despair inflicted by the atomic bombing and for continuously appealing for the abolition[5] of nuclear weapons. Based on the belief that nuclear weapons are an absolute evil that could bring about the annihilation of the human family race, he asserted that nothing is more important than for the people of the world to maintain a strong will to abolish nuclear weapons.

---

4) ［他動］超える ※［他動］は他動詞のこと、以下同じ   5) ［名］廃止、廃絶 ※［名］は名詞のこと、以下同じ

In the Peace Declaration of 2000, he looked back over the 20th century, dominated by war and the development of science and technology, and pleaded with the world to cut the chains of hatred[6] and violence to clear a path toward reconciliation[7].

The first Peace Declaration of the 21st Century (2001), appealed to the world to muster the courage to value reconciliation and humanity in order to make the 21st Century a nuclear-free one of peace and humanity. The 2004 Peace Declaration called for support of the Emergency Campaign to Ban Nuclear Weapons to eliminate all nuclear weapons from the face of the earth by 2020, the 75th anniversary of the atomic bombings.

With the aging of the A-bomb survivors, the number of people who are able to speak of their experiences of the bombing is continuing to decrease; considering this fact, Mayor Kazumi Matsui thought it important to have the people of future generations and the world share the experiences of the A-bomb survivors and their wish for peace, and for the first time in 2011, decided to directly include testimonies solicited from A-bomb survivors in the Peace Declaration. The 2015 declaration presented to policymakers and people of the world that "generosity" and "love for humanity" are the principles necessary to firm up one's belief in nuclear weapons abolition, which would then serve as motivation toward this goal.

6) [名]憎悪　7) [名]和解

So that no other people in the world would have to suffer tragedies like those experienced by Hiroshima and Nagasaki, Hiroshima will continue to plead in the Peace Declaration for the removal of nuclear weapons from the world and the establishment of lasting world peace.

CHAPTER 1
KAZUMI MATSUI's[1] PEACE DECLARATION
(2023–2011)

Peace Declaration (2023)

【A commentary by the City of Hiroshima】
Every year on August 6, the City of Hiroshima holds a Peace Memorial Ceremony to pray for the peaceful repose of the victims, for the abolition of nuclear weapons, and for lasting world peace. During that ceremony, the Mayor issues a Peace Declaration directed toward the world at large. As long as the need persists, Hiroshima's mayor will continue to issue these declarations calling for the elimination of nuclear weapons from the face of the earth. This is part of Hiroshima's effort to build a world of genuine and lasting world peace where no population will ever again experience the cruel devastation suffered by Hiroshima and Nagasaki.

"I want the leaders of all countries with nuclear weapons to visit Hiroshima and Nagasaki and, using their own eyes and ears, learn the realities of the atomic bombings—the lives lost in an instant, the bodies

---

1) 松井一實（市長任期2011年4月〜）

charred by heat rays; lives lost in agony[2] from burns and radiation[3], tended to by no one. I want them standing here to feel the full weight of the countless lives lost." The *hibakusha* making this plea was eight years old when the bomb exploded 78 years ago. He always remembered that day as a living hell.

The heads of state who attended the G7 Hiroshima Summit in May this year visited the Peace Memorial Museum, spoke with *hibakusha*, and wrote messages in the guestbook. Their messages provide proof that *hibakusha* pleas have reached them. As they stood before the Cenotaph for the A-bomb Victims[4], I conveyed the Spirit of Hiroshima underlying its inscription. Enduring past grief, overcoming hatred, we yearn for genuine world peace with all humanity living in harmony and prosperity. I believe our spirit is now engraved[5] in their hearts. And in this spirit, the first G7 Leaders' Hiroshima Vision on Nuclear Disarmament[6] reaffirms their "commitment to the ultimate goal of a world without nuclear weapons with undiminished[7] security for all," and declares that their "security policies are based on the understanding that nuclear weapons, for as long as they exist, should serve defensive purposes...."

However, leaders around the world must confront the reality that nuclear threats now being voiced by certain policymakers reveal the folly of nuclear deterrence theory[8]. They must immediately take concrete steps to lead us from the dangerous present

2) [名]激しい苦痛、苦悩   3) [名]放射線   4) Cenotaph for the A-bomb Victims原爆死没者慰霊碑   5) engrave[他動]深く刻み込む   6) G7 Leaders' Hiroshima Vision on Nuclear Disarmament核軍縮に関するG7首脳広島ビジ

toward our ideal world. In civil society, each of us must embrace the generosity and love for humanity embodied in the *hibakusha* message, "No one else should ever suffer as we have." It will be increasingly important for us to urge policymakers to abandon nuclear deterrence in favor of a peaceful world that refuses to compromise individual dignity[9] and security.

Mahatma Gandhi, who pursued independence for his native India through absolute nonviolence, asserted, "Non-violence is the greatest force at the disposal of [10] mankind. It is mightier than the mightiest weapon of destruction devised by the ingenuity of man.[11]" The UN General Assembly has adopted, as a formal document, a Programme of Action on a Culture of Peace[12]. To end the current war as quickly as possible, the leaders of nations should act in accordance with Gandhi's assertion and the Programme of Action, with civil society rising up in response.

To that end, it will be vital to build a social environment in which our dreams and hopes come alive in our daily lives through contact with or participation in music, art, sports, and other activities that transcend language, nationality, creed[13], and gender. And to create that social environment, let us promote initiatives to instill[14] the culture of peace everywhere. If we do, elected officials, who need the support of the people, will surely work with us toward a peaceful world.

The City of Hiroshima, together with more than

ョン　7）［形］衰えない、低下しない　※ with undiminished security for all すべ
ての者にとっての安全が損なわれない形で　※［形］は形容詞のこと、以下同じ　8）
nuclear deterrence theory　核抑止論 (NDT)　9）［名］尊厳　10) at the dis-

8,200 member cities of Mayors for Peace in 166 countries and regions, intends to promote the culture of peace globally through citizen-level exchange. Our goal is an environment in which our united desire for peace can reach the hearts of policymakers, helping to build an international community that maintains peace without relying on military force. We will continue to expand our programs to convey the realities of the atomic bombings to young people around the world so they can acquire the *hibakusha*'s passion for peace, spread it beyond national borders, and pass it on to future generations.

I ask all policymakers to follow in the footsteps of the leaders who attended the G7 Hiroshima Summit by visiting Hiroshima and sharing widely their desire for peace. I urge them to immediately cease all nuclear threats and turn toward a security regime[15] based on trust through dialogue in pursuit of civil society ideals.

I further urge the national government to heed the wishes of the *hibakusha* and the peace-loving Japanese people by reconciling[16] the differences between nuclear-weapon and non-nuclear-weapon states. Japan must immediately join the Treaty on the Prohibition of Nuclear Weapons (TPNW)[17] and establish common ground for discussions on nuclear weapons abolition by attending, at least as an observer, the Second Meeting of States Parties to the TPNW[18] to be held in November this year. The average age of the *hibakusha* now exceeds 85. The lives of many are still impaired[19] by radiation's

posal of~ 〜の自由になる、意のままになる 11) Non-violence is the greatest force at the disposal of mankind. It is mightier than the mightiest weapon of destruction devised by the ingenuity of man.「非暴力は人間に与えられた

harmful effects on mind and body. Thus, I demand that the Japanese government alleviate[20] their suffering through stronger support measures.

Today, at this Peace Memorial Ceremony commemorating 78 years since the bombing, we offer heartfelt condolences[21] to the souls of the atomic bomb victims. Together with Nagasaki and likeminded people around the world, we pledge to do everything in our power to abolish nuclear weapons and light the way toward lasting world peace.

*   *   *

Peace Declaration (2022)

【Comments by the City of Hiroshima】
〈Appealing that we must pursue the ideal of peace maintained without military force and render all nuclear buttons meaningless; quoting Leo Tolstoy's words to show that we must not tolerate self-centeredness that threatens others, even to the point of denying their existence; calling on leaders of nuclear powers to build bridges of trust among nations, and rather than treating a world without nuclear weapons like a distant dream, to take concrete steps toward its realization; declaring that Hiroshima will continue striding toward nuclear weapons abolition, and Mayors for Peace will encourage policymakers to pursue foreign policies through dialogue by promoting the culture of peace that rejects

最大の武器であり、人間が発明した最強の武器よりも強い力を持つ」というガンジーの格言　12) Programme of Action on a Culture of Peace平和の文化に関する行動計画　13)［名］信条、信念　14)［他動］根付かせる、染み込ませる

⟨all forms of violence; demanding that the Japanese government serve as mediator at the NPT Review Conference, participate in the next Meeting of States Parties to the TPNW, promptly become a State Party itself, and wholeheartedly support the movement toward nuclear weapons abolition as well as empathize with *hibakusha*'s suffering to better offer them enhanced support measures⟩

"I adored my mother; she raised me with such kindness and care." The woman speaking was 16 when she left home carrying the lunch her mother had lovingly prepared. She never imagined it would be their final parting. Summer, 77 years ago. That morning, without warning, the first nuclear weapon was dropped and detonated[22] over humanity. Standing near Hiroshima Station, the girl saw a terrifying flash. Then came a thunderous roar. Striking from behind, the blast blew her through the air and knocked her unconscious. When she came to, she wandered through the smoldering city, searching for her mother. She saw a horrifying number of blackened bodies. One charred[23] corpse[24] still stood, clinging to[25] the neck of a cow. Bodies floating in the river drifted up and down with the tide. She still remembers the morning when everyday life vanished violently into scenes from hell.

In invading Ukraine, the Russian leader, elected to protect the lives and property of his people, is using them as instruments of war, stealing the lives and

---

15) security regime安全保障体制   16) reconcile［他動］和解させる、仲裁する、調和させる   17) Treaty on the Prohibition of Nuclear Weapons (TPNW) 核兵器禁止条約   18) Second Meeting of States Parties to the TPNW   第

livelihoods of innocent civilians in another country. Around the world, the notion that peace depends on nuclear deterrence[26] gains momentum. These errors betray humanity's determination, born of our experiences of war, to achieve a peaceful world free from nuclear weapons. To accept the status quo[27] and abandon the ideal of peace maintained without military force is to threaten the very survival of the human race. We must stop repeating these mistakes. Above all, entrusting a nuclear button to any world leader is to sanction[28] continued nuclear threats to humanity and potential re-creation of the hellscape[29] of August 6, 1945. We must immediately render all nuclear buttons meaningless.

Must we keep tolerating self-centeredness that threatens others, even to the point of denying their existence? We should take to heart the words of Leo Tolstoy, the renowned Russian author of War and Peace, who advised, "Never build your happiness on the misfortune of others, for only in their happiness can you find your own."

Earlier this year, the five nuclear-weapon states issued a joint statement: "Nuclear war cannot be won and must never be fought." They further declared their intent to "...remain committed to our Nuclear Non-Proliferation Treaty (NPT)[30] obligations." Having issued such a statement, why do they not attempt to fulfill their promises? Why do some even hint at using nuclear weapons? The nuclear powers[31] must act now

---

2回核兵器禁止条約締約国会議　19) impair［他動］害する、損なう　20) alleviate［他動］軽減［緩和］する、和らげる　21)［名］お悔やみ　22) detonate［自動］爆発する　※［自動］は自動詞のこと、以下同じ　23)［形］黒焦げの　24)［名］死体、

to build bridges of trust among nations. Rather than treating a world without nuclear weapons like a distant dream, they should be taking concrete steps toward its realization. I call on the leaders of the nuclear-weapon states to visit the atomic-bombed cities where they can personally encounter the consequences of using nuclear weapons and strengthen their will to take these steps. I want them to understand that the only sure way to protect the lives and property of their people is to eliminate nuclear weapons. I fervently[32] hope that the leaders who attend the G7 Summit in Hiroshima next year will reach this conclusion.

With the *hibakusha*'s will to peace at our core, and inheriting the "never-give-up" spirit of *hibakusha* leader Tsuboi Sunao, who dedicated his life to the cause, Hiroshima will continue striding toward nuclear weapons abolition, however arduous[33] the path.

Mayors for Peace, now a network of 8,200 peace cities around the world, will hold its 10th General Conference in Hiroshima this year. That conference will work toward a civil society in which each and every citizen shares the conviction[34] that happy lives require an end to war, an end to armed conflict, and an end to life-threatening social discrimination. In that pursuit, we will intensify cooperation among our peace-minded member cities to promote a "culture of peace" that rejects all forms of violence. Mayors for Peace encourages policymakers to pursue foreign policies through dialogue without relying on nuclear deterrence.

遺体　25) clinging to~　～にしがみついて　26) nuclear deterrence　核抑止 27) status quo (ラテン語)現在の体制、現状　28)［名］制裁　29)［名］地獄絵 図　30) Nuclear Non-Proliferation Treaty　核不拡散条約 (核拡散防止条

This past June, the First Meeting of States Parties to the Treaty on the Prohibition of Nuclear Weapons (TPNW) adopted a declaration that, against the backdrop of the Russian invasion, categorically rejects the threat of nuclear weapons. With nuclear weapons-dependent states participating as observers, the meeting specifically stressed that the TPNW contributes to and complements the NPT. Therefore, I demand first that the Japanese government serve as mediator at the NPT Review Conference[35]. Then, Japan must participate in the next Meeting of States Parties to the TPNW, promptly become a State Party itself, and wholeheartedly support the movement toward nuclear weapons abolition.

The average age of the *hibakusha* now exceeds 84, and their lives are still impaired by radiation's adverse effects on their minds and bodies. Thus, I further demand that the Japanese government empathize with their suffering to better offer them enhanced support measures.

Today, at this Peace Memorial Ceremony commemorating 77 years since the bombing, we offer heartfelt condolences to the souls of the atomic bomb victims. Together with Nagasaki and likeminded people around the world, we pledge to do everything in our power to abolish nuclear weapons and light the way toward lasting world peace.

*   *   *

約)　31) The nuclear powers　核保有国　32)［副］熱烈に ※［副］は副詞のこと、以下同じ　33)［形］困難な　34)［名］信念、思い
35) NPT Review Conference 核不拡散条約再検討会議

Peace Declaration (2021)

【Comments by the City of Hiroshima】
〈Calling on world leaders to aim a sustainable world free from nuclear weapons based on the TPNW; appealing that the combined wisdom of all peoples must be trained on the total abolition of such weapons, and urging young people to take action; declaring the will to create an environment to urge world leaders to shift their policies by promoting a "culture of peace" to make the call to abolish such weapons become the general consensus[36] of civil society; demanding that world leaders shift toward security based on trust derived from dialogue; urging the Japanese government to sign and ratify the TPNW, participate in the first Meeting of States Parties, and fulfill the role of mediator between the nuclear and non-nuclear weapons states, and demanding immediate relief for those exposed to the black rain〉

On this day 76 years ago, a single atomic bomb instantly reduced our hometown to a scorched plain. That bombing brought cruel death to countless innocent victims and left those who managed to survive with profound[37], lifelong physical and emotional injuries due to radiation, fear of aftereffects, and economic hardship. One survivor who gave birth to a girl soon after the bombing says, "As more horrors of the bomb came to light, and I became more concerned

36) [名]総意、民意　37) [形]深い

about their effects, I worried less about myself and more about my child. Imagining the future awaiting my daughter, my suffering grew, night after sleepless night."

"No one else should ever suffer as we have." These words express the will of survivors who, having known horrors too painful to recall, were condemned to fear, frustration, and agony by the likely future of their children and their own irradiated[38] bodies. When *hibakusha* tell their stories, they convey not only the horror and inhumanity of nuclear weapons but also an intense yearning[39] for peace, born of compassion[40]. Finally, after 75 long years of sustained activity, their demands have moved the international community. This year, on January 22, the Treaty on the Prohibition of Nuclear Weapons (TPNW) entered into effect. It remains now for world leaders to support this treaty, shifting their focus toward a truly sustainable society free from nuclear weapons.

The novel coronavirus still ravages[41] our world. The community of nations recognizes this threat to humanity and is taking urgent measures to end it. Nuclear weapons, developed to win wars, are a threat of total annihilation[42] that we can certainly end, if all nations work together. No sustainable society is possible with these weapons continually poised for indiscriminate slaughter[43]. The combined wisdom of all peoples must be trained on their total abolition.

The road to abolition will not be smooth, but a ray of hope shines from the young people now taking up the

---

38)［形］放射線を浴びた　39)［名］切ない思い、熱望　40)［名］思いやり、深い同情　41) ravage［他動］ひどく破壊する　42)［名］全滅、絶滅　43)［名］大量殺戮、虐殺

hibakusha's quest. One survivor who witnessed hell that day entrusts our future to the young with these words: "Start small, but start. I hope each of you will do whatever you can to promote and maintain the treasure we call peace." I ask our young to sustain an unshakeable conviction that nuclear weapons are incompatible with full, healthy lives for their loved ones. I further ask them to share that conviction persuasively with people around the world.

We must never forget that young people can certainly compel world leaders to turn away from nuclear deterrence. Three years after the bombing, Helen Keller visited Hiroshima, encouraging its residents in the struggle to recover. "Alone we can do so little. Together we can do so much." Her words remind us that individuals, when united, have the power to change the world. If the determination to live in peace sweeps through civil society, people will elect leaders who share that determination. Nuclear weapons are the ultimate human violence. If civil society decides to live without them, the door to a nuclear-weapon-free world will open wide. The atomic bombed city of Hiroshima will never stop preserving the facts of the bombing, disseminating[44] them beyond borders, and conveying them to the future. With the more than 8,000 Mayors for Peace member cities in 165 countries and regions, we will promote a worldwide "culture of peace." In a global culture where peace is a universal value, world leaders will find the courage to correct their policies.

---

44) disseminate［他動］広める

Given the uncertainty concerning nuclear weapons derived from stalled disarmament negotiations, I have an urgent demand to make of world leaders. The time has come for a profound tactical shift away from reliance on threats toward security based on trust derived from dialogue. Experience has taught humanity that threatening others for self-defense benefits no one. Our leaders must understand that threatening rivals with nuclear weapons achieves nothing of value, but treating each other with empathy and building long-lasting friendships connect directly to national self-interest. To that end, I urge all world leaders to visit Hiroshima and Nagasaki, achieve a deeper understanding of the bombings, fulfill the disarmament mandate of the Nuclear Non-Proliferation Treaty, and join the discussions aimed at maximizing the effectiveness of the TPNW.

With respect to the Japanese government, I request productive mediation between the nuclear and non-nuclear weapon states. Furthermore, in accordance with the will of the *hibakusha*, I demand immediate signing and ratification[45] of the TPNW, then constructive participation in the first Meeting of States Parties. Fulfilling the role of mediator must involve creating an environment that facilitates the restoration of international trust and security without reliance on nuclear weapons. The average age of our *hibakusha* is close to 84. I demand more generous assistance for them and the many others suffering daily due to the

45) [名]批准

harmful physical and emotional effects of radiation. I demand as well immediate relief for those exposed to the black rain.

At this Peace Memorial Ceremony marking 76 years since the bombing, we offer heartfelt prayers for the peaceful repose[46] of the souls of the atomic bomb victims. Together with Nagasaki and likeminded people around the world, we pledge to do everything in our power to abolish nuclear weapons and light the way toward lasting world peace.

＊　＊　＊

Peace Declaration (2020)

【Comments by the City of Hiroshima】
〈Calling on the civil society to unite against a new threat of the novel coronavirus through learning from the tragedies of the past; quoting words of a *hibakusha*, Pope Francis, and Ogata Sadako to highlight the importance of solidarity; asserting that Hiroshima considers it our duty to build in civil society a consensus that the people of the world must unite to achieve nuclear weapons abolition and lasting world peace; urging world leaders to strengthen their determination to make the framework of the NPT and TPNW function effectively; urging the Japanese government to become a party to the TPNW and persuade the global public to unite with the spirit of Hiroshima and demanding the

46) [名]休息※ peaceful repose 冥福

political decision to expand the "black rain areas"⟩

On August 6, 1945, a single atomic bomb destroyed our city. Rumor at the time had it that "nothing will grow here for 75 years." And yet, Hiroshima recovered, becoming a symbol of peace visited by millions from around the world.

Humanity struggles now against a new threat: the novel coronavirus. However, with what we have learned from the tragedies of the past, we should be able to overcome this threat.

When the 1918 flu pandemic attacked a century ago, it took tens of millions of lives and terrorized the world because nations fighting World War I were unable to meet the threat together. A subsequent upsurge[47] in nationalism led to World War II and the atomic bombings.

We must never allow this painful past to repeat itself. Civil society must reject self-centered nationalism and unite against all threats.

The day after the atomic bombing, a young boy of 13 saw, "...victims lying in rows on the bridge. Many were injured. Many had breathed their last. Most were burned, their skin hanging off. Many were begging, 'Water! Give me water!'" Long after that horrifying experience, the man asserts, "Fighting happens when people think only of themselves or their own countries."

Last November, when Pope Francis visited our city, he left us with a powerful message: "To remember, to

---

47) ［名］台頭

journey together, to protect. These are three moral imperatives.[48)]"

Ogata Sadako, as UN High Commissioner for Refugees, worked passionately to assist those in need. She spoke from experience when she said, "The important thing is to save the lives of those who are suffering. No country can live in peace alone. The world is connected."

These messages urge us to unite against threats to humanity and avoid repeating our tragic past.

Hiroshima is what it is today because our predecessor[49)]s cared about each other; they stood together through their ordeal. Visitors from other countries leave the Peace Memorial Museum with comments like, "Now we see this tragedy as our own," and "This is a lesson for the future of humanity." Hiroshima considers it our duty to build in civil society a consensus that the people of the world must unite to achieve nuclear weapons abolition and lasting world peace.

Turning to the United Nations, the Nuclear Non-Proliferation Treaty (NPT), which went into effect 50 years ago, and the Treaty on the Prohibition of Nuclear Weapons (TPNW) adopted three years ago are both critical to eliminating nuclear weapons. They comprise a framework that we must pass on to future generations, yet their future is opaque[50)]. Now more than ever, world leaders must strengthen their determination to make this framework function effectively.

---

48) [名]必要事項、命令、責務   49) [名]先人   50) [形]不透明な

That is precisely why I urge them to visit Hiroshima and deepen their understanding of the atomic bombing. I further urge them to invest fully in the NPT Review Conference. They must negotiate in good faith toward nuclear disarmament, as stipulated by the NPT, and continue constructive dialogue toward a security system free from reliance on nuclear weapons.

To enhance its role as mediator between the nuclear-weapon and non-nuclear-weapon states, I ask the Japanese government to heed[51] the appeal of the *hibakusha* that it sign and ratify, and become a party to the TPNW. As the only nation to suffer a nuclear attack, Japan must persuade the global public to unite with the spirit of Hiroshima. I further demand more generous assistance for the *hibakusha*, whose average age exceeds 83, and the many others whose daily lives are still plagued[52] by suffering due to the harmful effects of radiation on their minds and bodies. And once more, I demand the political decision to expand the "black rain areas."

At this Peace Memorial Ceremony marking 75 years since the bombing, we offer heartfelt prayers for the peaceful repose of the souls of the atomic bomb victims. Together with Nagasaki and likeminded people around the world, we pledge to do everything in our power to abolish nuclear weapons and open a path to genuine and lasting world peace.

＊　　＊　　＊

51) heed［他動］心に留める　52) plague［他動］苦しめる

Peace Declaration (2019)

【Comments by the City of Hiroshima】
〈Urging to recall that our elders pursued an ideal, a world beyond war, and undertook to construct a system of international cooperation; including two *hibakusha*'s experiences and quoting a *tanka* poem by a *hibakusha* for the first time; appealing for "tolerance" to achieve a peaceful, sustainable world by introducing Mahatma Gandhi's words; calling on coming generations not to dismiss the atomic bombings and the war as mere events of the past; calling on world leaders to move forward with civil society and remember the US and USSR predecessors manifested reason and turned to dialogue to seek disarmament; urging the national government to accede to the *hibakusha*'s request that the TPNW signed and ratified and display leadership in taking the next step toward a world free from nuclear weapons〉

Around the world today, we see self-centered nationalism in ascendance[53], tensions heightened by international exclusivity and rivalry, with nuclear disarmament at a standstill. What are we to make of these global phenomena? Having undergone two world wars, our elders pursued an ideal—a world beyond war. They undertook to construct a system of international cooperation. Should we not now recall and, for human survival, strive for that ideal world? I ask this especially

---

53) [名]優位

of you, the youth who have never known war but will lead the future. For this purpose, I ask you to listen carefully to the *hibakusha* of August 6, 1945.

A woman who was five then has written this poem:

Little sister with a bowl cut / head spraying blood embraced by Mother / turned raging Asura

A youth of 18 saw this: "They were nearly naked, their clothes burned to tatters[54], but I couldn't tell the men from the women. Hair gone, eyeballs popped out, lips and ears ripped off, skin hanging from faces, bodies covered in blood—and so many." Today he insists, "We must never, ever allow this to happen to any future generation. We are enough." Appeals like these come from survivors who carry deep scars in body and soul. Are they reaching you?

"A single person is small and weak, but if each of us seeks peace, I'm sure we can stop the forces pushing for war." This woman was 15 at the time. Can we allow her faith to end up an empty wish?

Turning to the world, we do see that individuals have little power, but we also see many examples of the combined strength of multitudes[55] achieving their goal. Indian independence is one such example. Mahatma Gandhi, who contributed to that independence through personal pain and suffering, left us these words, "Intolerance[56] is itself a form of violence and an obstacle to the growth of a true democratic

---

54) [名]ぼろきれ　55) [名]大勢の人　56) [名]不寛容

spirit." To confront our current circumstances and achieve a peaceful, sustainable world, we must transcend differences of status or opinion and strive together in a spirit of tolerance toward our ideal. To accomplish this, coming generations must never dismiss the atomic bombings and the war as mere events of the past. It is vital that they internalize the progress the *hibakusha* and others have made toward a peaceful world, then drive steadfastly forward.

World leaders must move forward with them, advancing civil society's ideal. This is why I urge them to visit the atomic-bombed cities, listen to the *hibakusha*, and tour the Peace Memorial Museum and the National Peace Memorial Hall to face what actually happened in the lives of individual victims and their loved ones. I want our current leaders to remember their courageous predecessors: when nuclear superpowers, the US and USSR, were engaged in a tense, escalating nuclear arms race, their leaders manifested reason and turned to dialogue to seek disarmament.

This city, along with the nearly 7,800 member cities of Mayors for Peace, is spreading the Spirit of Hiroshima throughout civil society to create an environment supportive of leaders taking action for nuclear abolition. We want leaders around the world to pursue negotiations in good faith on nuclear disarmament, as mandated by Article VI of the Nuclear Non-Proliferation Treaty, and respond to the yearning of civil society for entry into force of the Treaty on the Prohibition of Nuclear Weapons (TPNW), a milestone on the road to a nuclear-weapon-free world.

I call on the government of the only country to experience a nuclear weapon in war to accede to[57] the hibakusha's request that the TPNW be signed and ratified. I urge Japan's leaders to manifest the pacifism[58] of the Japanese Constitution by displaying leadership in taking the next step toward a world free from nuclear weapons. Furthermore, I demand policies that expand the "black rain areas" and improve assistance to the hibakusha, whose average age exceeds 82, as well as the many others whose minds, bodies and daily lives are still plagued by suffering due to the harmful effects of radiation.

Today, at this Peace Memorial Ceremony commemorating 74 years since the atomic bombing, we offer our heartfelt consolation[59] to the souls of the atomic bomb victims and, in concert with the city of Nagasaki and kindred[60] spirits around the world, we pledge to make every effort to achieve the total elimination of nuclear weapons and beyond that, a world of genuine, lasting peace.

＊　　　＊　　　＊

---

57) accede to~ ～に応じる　58) [名]平和主義　59) [名]慰め　60) [形]親族
の、同類の※ kindred spirits 思いを同じくする人々

Peace Declaration (2018)

【Comments by the City of Hiroshima】

〈Presenting "reason" and "continuation" as the principles necessary to strengthen one's belief in nuclear weapons abolition; including two A-bomb survivors' experiences relevant; pointing out that the ICAN won the Nobel Peace Prize and the spirit of the *hibakusha* is spreading through the world, but certain countries are blatantly[61] proclaiming[62] self-centered nationalism, rekindling[63] tensions that had eased with the end of the Cold War; appealing for continuous talking about *Hiroshima*, and efforts to eliminate nuclear weapons based on intelligent actions by leaders around the world; appealing that the approach of nuclear deterrence and nuclear umbrellas is unstable and dangerous, thus calling on world leaders to negotiate in good faith the elimination of nuclear arsenals and to strive to make the TPNW a milestone along the path to a nuclear-weapon-free world; calling on the Japanese government to play its role in the movement toward the entry into force of the TPNW to lead the international community toward dialogue and cooperation for a world without nuclear weapons〉

It's 73 years ago and a Monday morning, just like today. With the mid-summer sun already blazing, Hiroshima starts another day. Please listen to what I say next as if you and your loved ones were there. At 8:15

---

61) ［副］明らかに　露骨に　62) proclaim［他動］公表 (宣言) する　63) rekindle［他動］再燃させる

comes a blinding flash. A fireball more than a million degrees Celsius releases intense radiation, heat, and then, a tremendous blast. Below the roiling mushroom cloud, innocent lives are snuffed out[64] as the city is obliterated[65].

"I'm so hot! It's killing me!" From under collapsed houses, children scream for their mothers. "Water! Please, water!" come moans[66] and groans[67] from the brink of death. In the foul stench[68] of burning people, victims wander around like ghosts, their flesh peeled and red. Black rain fell all around. The scenes of hell burnt into their memories and the radiation eating away at their minds and bodies are even now sources of pain for *hibakusha* who survive.

Today, with more than 14,000 nuclear warheads remaining, the likelihood is growing that what we saw in Hiroshima after the explosion that day will return, by intent or accident, plunging[69] people into agony.

The *hibakusha*, based on their intimate knowledge of the terror of nuclear weapons, are ringing an alarm against the temptation to possess them. Year by year, as *hibakusha* decrease in number, listening to them grows ever more crucial. One *hibakusha* who was 20 says, "If nuclear weapons are used, every living thing will be annihilated. Our beautiful Earth will be left in ruins. World leaders should gather in the A-bombed cities, encounter our tragedy, and, at a minimum, set a course toward freedom from nuclear weapons. I want human beings to become good stewards of creation capable of

---

64) snuff out 殺す 65) obliterate［他動］完全に破壊する 66)［名］うめき声
67)［名］うなり声 68)［名］悪臭 69) plunge［他動］陥れる

abolishing nuclear weapons." He asks world leaders to focus their reason and insight on abolishing nuclear weapons so we can treasure life and avoid destroying the Earth.

Last year, the Nobel Peace Prize went to ICAN, an organization that contributed to the formation of the Treaty on the Prohibition of Nuclear Weapons. Thus, the spirit of the *hibakusha* is spreading through the world. On the other hand, certain countries are blatantly proclaiming self-centered nationalism and modernizing their nuclear arsenals, rekindling tensions that had eased with the end of the Cold War.

Another *hibakusha* who was 20 makes this appeal: "I hope no such tragedy ever happens again. We must never allow ours to fade into the forgotten past. I hope from the bottom of my heart that humanity will apply our wisdom to making our entire Earth peaceful." If the human family forgets history or stops confronting it, we could again commit a terrible error. That is precisely why we must continue talking about Hiroshima. Efforts to eliminate nuclear weapons must continue based on intelligent actions by leaders around the world.

Nuclear deterrence and nuclear umbrellas flaunt the destructive power of nuclear weapons and seek to maintain international order by generating fear in rival countries. This approach to guaranteeing long-term security is inherently unstable and extremely dangerous. World leaders must have this reality etched[70] in their

---

70) etch[他動] (心に) 刻み込む

hearts as they negotiate in good faith the elimination of nuclear arsenals, which is a legal obligation under the Nuclear Non-Proliferation Treaty. Furthermore, they must strive to make the Treaty on the Prohibition of Nuclear Weapons a milestone along the path to a nuclear-weapon-free world.

We in civil society hope that the easing of tensions on the Korean Peninsula will proceed through peaceable dialogue. For leaders to take courageous actions, civil society must respect diversity, build mutual trust, and make the abolition of nuclear weapons a value shared by all humankind. Mayors for Peace, now with more than 7,600 member cities around the world, will focus on creating that environment.

I ask the Japanese government to manifest the magnificent pacifism of the Japanese Constitution in the movement toward the entry into force of the Treaty on the Prohibition of Nuclear Weapons by playing its proper role, leading the international community toward dialogue and cooperation for a world without nuclear weapons. In addition, I hereby demand an expansion of the black rain areas along with greater concern and improved assistance for the many people suffering the mental and physical effects of radiation, especially the *hibakusha*, whose average age is now over 82.

Today, we renew our commitment and offer sincere consolation to the souls of all A-bomb victims. Along with Nagasaki, the other A-bombed city, and with much of the world's population, Hiroshima pledges to do everything in our power to achieve lasting world peace and the abolition of nuclear weapons.

* * *

Peace Declaration (2017)

【Comments by the City of Hiroshima】

〈Presenting "conscience" and "in good faith" as the principles necessary to strengthen one's belief in nuclear weapons abolition, which would then serve as motivation toward this goal; including two A-bomb survivors' experiences relevant to this topic; touching upon the adoption of the Treaty on the Prohibition of Nuclear Weapons (TPNW) with support from 122 countries; calling on nations to advance efforts toward a world without nuclear weapons; calling on the Japanese government to do everything in its power to bridge the gap between the nuclear-weapon and non-nuclear-weapon states, thereby facilitating the ratification of the TPNW; encouraging people to visit Hiroshima to take to heart the *hibakusha*'s wish for nuclear abolition, to broaden the circle of empathy to the entire world; calling on young visitors to expand the circle of friendship as ambassadors for nuclear abolition〉

Friends, seventy-two years ago today, on August 6, at 8:15 a.m., absolute evil was unleashed[71] in the sky over

---

71) unleash［他動］放つ

Hiroshima. Let's imagine for a moment what happened under that roiling mushroom cloud. *Pika*—the penetrating flash, extreme radiation and heat. *Don*—the earth-shattering roar and blast. As the blackness lifts, the scenes emerging into view reveal countless scattered corpses charred beyond recognition even as man or woman. Stepping between the corpses, badly burned, nearly naked figures with blackened faces, singed hair, and tattered[72], dangling[73] skin wander through spreading flames, looking for water. The rivers in front of you are filled with bodies; the riverbanks so crowded with burnt, half-naked victims you have no place to step. This is truly hell. Under that mushroom cloud, the absolutely evil atomic bomb brought gruesome[74] death to vast numbers of innocent civilians and left those it didn't kill with deep physical and emotional scars, including the aftereffects of radiation and endless health fears. Giving rise to social discrimination and prejudice, it devastated even the lives of those who managed to survive.

This hell is not a thing of the past. As long as nuclear weapons exist and policymakers threaten their use, their horror could leap into our present at any moment. You could find yourself suffering their cruelty[75].

This is why I ask everyone to listen to the voices of the *hibakusha*. A man who was 15 at the time says, "When I recall the friends and acquaintances[76] I saw dying in those scenes of hell, I can barely endure the pain." Then, appealing to us all, he asks, "To know the blessing of

---

72) tatter［他動］ずたずたに裂く　73) dangle［自動］垂れ下がる
74)［形］むごたらしい　75)［名］むごたらしさ、残虐な行為
76)［名］知り合い

being alive, to treat everyone with compassion, love, and respect—are these not steps to world peace?"

Another *hibakusha* who was 17 says, "I ask the leaders of the nuclear-armed states to prevent the destruction of this planet by abandoning nuclear deterrence and abolishing immediately all atomic and hydrogen bombs. Then they must work wholeheartedly to preserve our irreplaceable Earth for future generations."

Friends, this appeal to conscience and this demand that policymakers respond conscientiously[77] are deeply rooted in the *hibakusha* experience. Let's all make their appeal and demand our own, spread them throughout the world, and pass them on to the next generation.

Policymakers, I ask you especially to respect your differences and make good-faith efforts to overcome them. To this end, it is vital that you deepen your awareness of the inhumanity of nuclear weapons, consider the perspectives[78] of other countries, and recognize your duty to build a world where all thrive together.

Civil society fully understands that nuclear weapons are useless for national security. The dangers involved in controlling nuclear materials are widely understood. Today, a single bomb can wield[79] thousands of times the destructive power of the bombs dropped 72 years ago. Any use of such weapons would plunge the entire world into hell, the user as well as the enemy. Humankind must never commit such an act. Thus, we can accurately say that possessing nuclear weapons

---

77) [副]誠実に　78) [名]考え方、視点　79) wield[他動]振るう

means nothing more than spending enormous sums of money to endanger all humanity.

Peace Memorial Park is now drawing over 1.7 million visitors a year from around the world, but I want even more visitors to see the realities of the bombing and listen to survivor testimony. I want them to understand what happened under the mushroom cloud, take to heart the survivors' desire to eliminate nuclear weapons and broaden the circle of empathy to the entire world. In particular, I want more youthful visitors expanding the circle of friendship as ambassadors for nuclear abolition. I assure you that Hiroshima will continue to bring people together for these purposes and inspire them to take action.

Mayors for Peace, led by Hiroshima, now comprises over 7,400 city members around the world. We work within civil society to create an environment that helps policymakers move beyond national borders to act in good faith and conscience for the abolition of nuclear weapons.

In July, when 122 United Nations members, not including the nuclear-weapon and nuclear-umbrella states, adopted the Treaty on the Prohibition of Nuclear Weapons, they demonstrated their unequivocal[80] determination to achieve abolition. Given this development, the governments of all countries must now strive to advance further toward a nuclear-weapon-free world.

The Japanese Constitution states, "We, the Japanese

---

80) ［形］明白な

people, pledge our national honor to accomplish these high ideals and purposes with all our resources." Therefore, I call especially on the Japanese government to manifest the pacifism in our constitution by doing everything in its power to bridge the gap between the nuclear-weapon and non-nuclear-weapon states, thereby facilitating the ratification of the Treaty on the Prohibition of Nuclear Weapons. I further demand more compassionate[81] government assistance to the *hibakusha*, whose average age is now over 81, and to the many others also suffering mentally and physically from the effects of radiation, along with expansion of the "black rain areas."

We offer heartfelt prayers for the repose of the atomic bomb victims and pledge to work with the people of the world to do all in our power to bring lasting peace and free ourselves from the absolute evil that is nuclear weapons.

*   *   *

Peace Declaration (2016)

【Comments by the City of Hiroshima】
⟨Presenting "passion" and "unity" as the principles necessary to strengthen one's belief in nuclear weapons abolition, which would then serve as motivation toward this goal; including two A-bomb survivors' experiences relevant to this topic; quoting part of US President

---

81) ［形］思いやりのある

Obama's speech, "… among those nations like my own that hold nuclear stockpiles, we must have the courage to escape the logic of fear, and pursue a world without them," which was given during his visit to Hiroshima; once again urging policymakers of the world to visit the A-bombed cities, and expressed support for young people in starting to take action; expressing expectations for Prime Minister Abe to display leadership with President Obama; pointing out that a legal framework banning nuclear weapons was indispensable to realize a nuclear-weapon-free world⟩

1945, August 6, 8:15 a.m. Slicing through the clear blue sky, a previously unknown "absolute evil" is unleashed on Hiroshima, instantly searing the entire city. Koreans, Chinese, Southeast Asians, American prisoners of war, children, the elderly and other innocent people are slaughtered[82]. By the end of the year, 140,000 are dead.

Those who managed to survive suffered the aftereffects of radiation, encountered discrimination in work and marriage, and still carry deep scars in their minds and bodies. From utter obliteration, Hiroshima was reborn a beautiful city of peace; but familiar scenes from our riversides, patterns of daily life, and cultural traditions nurtured through centuries of history vanished in that "absolute evil," never to return.

He was a boy of 17. Today he recalls, "Charred corpses blocked the road. An eerie[83] stench filled my nose. A

---

82) slaughter[他動]虐殺する　83) [形]異常な

sea of fire spread as far as I could see. Hiroshima was a living hell." She was a girl of 18. "I was covered in blood. Around me were people with skin flayed from their backs hanging all the way to their feet—crying, screaming, begging for water."

Seventy-one years later, over 15,000 nuclear weapons remain, individually much more destructive than the one that inflicted Hiroshima's tragedy, collectively enough to destroy the Earth itself. We now know of numerous accidents and incidents that brought us to the brink of nuclear explosions or war; today we even fear their use by terrorists.

Given this reality, we must heed the *hibakusha*. The man who described a living hell says, "For the future of humanity, we need to help each other live in peace and happiness with reverence for all life." The woman who was covered in blood appeals to coming generations, "To make the most of the life we've been given, please, everyone, shout loudly that we don't need nuclear weapons." If we accept these appeals, we must do far more than we have been doing. We must respect diverse values and strive persistently toward a world where all people are truly "living together."

When President Obama visited Hiroshima in May, he became the first sitting president of the country that dropped the atomic bomb to do so. Declaring, "... among those nations like my own that hold nuclear stockpiles[84], we must have the courage to escape the logic of fear, and pursue a world without them," he

---

84) nuclear stockpiles 核備蓄

expressed acceptance of the *hibakusha*'s heartfelt plea that "no one else should ever suffer as we have." Demonstrating to the people of the U.S. and the world a passion to fight to eliminate all remaining nuclear weapons, the President's words showed that he was touched by the spirit of Hiroshima, which refuses to accept the "absolute evil."

Is it not time to honor the spirit of Hiroshima and clear the path toward a world free from that "absolute evil," that ultimate inhumanity? Is it not time to unify and manifest our passion in action? This year, for the first time ever, the G7 foreign ministers gathered in Hiroshima. Transcending the differences between countries with and without nuclear weapons, their declaration called for political leaders to visit Hiroshima and Nagasaki, for early entry into force of the Comprehensive Nuclear-Test-Ban Treaty, and fulfillment of the obligation to negotiate nuclear disarmament mandated by the Nuclear Non-Proliferation Treaty. This declaration was unquestionably a step toward unity.

We need to fill our policymakers with the passion to solidify this unity and create a security system based on trust and dialogue. To that end, I once again urge the leaders of all nations to visit the A-bombed cities. As President Obama confirmed in Hiroshima, such visits will surely etch the reality of the atomic bombings in each heart. Along with conveying the pain and suffering of the *hibakusha*, I am convinced they will elicit[85] manifestations[86] of determination.

---

85) elicit［他動］導き出す　86) ［名］表明

The average age of the *hibakusha* has exceeded 80. Our time to hear their experiences face to face grows short. Looking toward the future, we will need our youth to help convey the words and feelings of the *hibakusha*. Mayors for Peace, now with over 7,000 city members worldwide, will work regionally, through more than 20 lead cities, and globally, led by Hiroshima and Nagasaki, to promote youth exchange. We will help young people cultivate a shared determination to stand together and initiate concrete action for the abolition of nuclear weapons.

Here in Hiroshima, Prime Minister Abe expressed determination "to realize a world free of nuclear weapons." I expect him to join with President Obama and display leadership in this endeavor[87]. A nuclear-weapon-free-world would manifest the noble pacifism of the Japanese Constitution, and to ensure progress, a legal framework banning nuclear weapons is indispensable[88]. In addition, I demand that the Japanese government expand the "black rain areas" and improve assistance to the *hibakusha*, whose average age is over 80, and the many others who suffer the mental and physical effects of radiation.

Today, we renew our determination, offer heartfelt consolation to the souls of the A-bomb victims, and pledge to do everything in our power, working with the A-bombed city of Nagasaki and millions around the world, to abolish nuclear weapons and build lasting world peace.

---

87) [名] 努力　88) [形] 絶対に必要な

＊　　＊　　＊

Peace Declaration (2015)

【Comments by the City of Hiroshima】
〈Presenting "generosity" and "love for humanity" as the principles necessary to firm up one's belief in nuclear weapons abolition, which would then serve as motivation toward this goal; included two A-bomb survivors' experiences relevant to this topic; calling on everyone to contemplate the nuclear problem as their own, because as long as nuclear weapons exist, anyone could become a *hibakusha* at any time; urging policymakers of the world to visit the A-bombed cities and to create broadly versatile security systems that do not depend on military might; pledging to strive toward negotiations for a nuclear weapons convention and abolition of nuclear weapons by 2020; calling on the Japanese government, in its role as bridge between the nuclear- and non-nuclear-weapon states, to guide all states toward these discussions; offering Hiroshima as the venue for dialogue and outreach〉

In our town, we had the warmth of family life, the deep human bonds of community, festivals heralding[89] each season, traditional culture and buildings passed down through history, as well as riversides where children played. At 8:15 a.m., August 6, 1945, all of that was destroyed by a single atomic bomb. Below the

---

89) herald［他動］到来を告げる

mushroom cloud, a charred mother and child embraced, countless corpses floated in rivers, and buildings burned to the ground. Tens of thousands were burned in those flames. By year's end, 140,000 irreplaceable lives had been taken, that number including Koreans, Chinese, Southeast Asians, and American prisoners of war.

Those who managed to survive, their lives grotesquely distorted, were left to suffer serious physical and emotional aftereffects compounded by discrimination and prejudice. Children stole or fought routinely to survive. A young boy rendered an A-bomb orphan still lives alone; a wife was divorced when her exposure was discovered. The suffering continues.

"*Madotekure!*" This is the heartbroken cry of *hibakusha* who want Hiroshima—their hometown, their families, their own minds and bodies—put back the way it was.

One hundred years after opening as the Hiroshima Prefectural Commercial Exhibition Hall and 70 years after the atomic bombing, the A-bomb Dome still watches over Hiroshima. In front of this witness to history, I want us all, once again, to face squarely what the A-bomb did and embrace fully the spirit of the *hibakusha*.

Meanwhile, our world still bristles with[90] more than 15,000 nuclear weapons, and policymakers in the nuclear-armed states remain trapped in provincial thinking, repeating by word and deed their nuclear

---

90) bristle with~ 〜でいっぱいである

intimidation[91]. We now know about the many incidents and accidents that have taken us to the brink of nuclear war or nuclear explosions. Today, we worry as well about nuclear terrorism.

As long as nuclear weapons exist, anyone could become a *hibakusha* at any time. If that happens, the damage will reach indiscriminately beyond national borders. People of the world, please listen carefully to the words of the *hibakusha* and, profoundly accepting the spirit of Hiroshima, contemplate[92] the nuclear problem as your own.

A woman who was 16 at the time appeals, "Expanding ever wider the circle of harmony that includes your family, friends, and neighbors links directly to world peace. Empathy, kindness, solidarity—these are not just intellectual concepts; we have to feel them in our bones." A man who was 12 emphasizes, "War means tragedy for adults and children alike. Empathy, caring, loving others and oneself—this is where peace comes from."

These heartrending messages, forged[93] in a cauldron[94] of suffering and sorrow, transcend hatred and rejection. Their spirit is generosity and love for humanity; their focus is the future of humankind.

Human beings transcend differences of nationality, race, religion, and language to live out our one-time-only lives on the planet we share. To coexist we must abolish the absolute evil and ultimate inhumanity that is nuclear weapons. Now is the time to start taking

91) ［名］威嚇 92) contemplate ［他動］熟考する 93) forge ［他動］築き上げる
94) ［名］大釜 ※ in a cauldron of suffering and sorrow つらく悲しい境遇の中
で

action. Young people are already starting petition drives, posting messages, organizing marches and launching a variety of efforts. Let's all work together to build an enormous ground swell[95].

In this milestone 70th year, the average *hibakusha* is now over 80 years old. The city of Hiroshima will work even harder to preserve the facts of the bombing, disseminate them to the world, and convey them to coming generations. At the same time, as president of Mayors for Peace, now with more than 6,700 member cities, Hiroshima will act with determination, doing everything in our power to accelerate the international trend toward negotiations for a nuclear weapons convention and abolition of nuclear weapons by 2020.

Is it not the policymakers' proper role to pursue happiness for their own people based on generosity and love of humanity? Policymakers meeting tirelessly to talk—this is the first step toward nuclear weapons abolition. The next step is to create, through the trust thus won, broadly versatile security systems that do not depend on military might. Working with patience and perseverance[96] to achieve those systems will be vital, and will require that we promote throughout the world the path to true peace revealed by the pacifism of the Japanese Constitution.

The summit meeting to be held in Japan's Ise-Shima next year and the foreign ministers' meeting to be held in Hiroshima prior to that summit are perfect opportunities to deliver a message about the abolition

---

95) ground swell うねり 96) [名]不屈の努力

of nuclear weapons. President Obama and other policymakers, please come to the A-bombed cities, hear the *hibakusha* with your own ears, and encounter the reality of the atomic bombings. Surely, you will be impelled to start discussing a legal framework, including a nuclear weapons convention.

We call on the Japanese government, in its role as bridge between the nuclear- and non-nuclear-weapon states, to guide all states toward these discussions, and we offer Hiroshima as the venue for dialogue and outreach[97]. In addition, we ask that greater compassion for our elderly *hibakusha* and the many others who now suffer the effects of radiation be expressed through stronger support measures. In particular, we demand expansion of the "black rain areas."

Offering our heartfelt prayers for the peaceful repose of the A-bomb victims, we express as well our gratitude to the *hibakusha* and all our predecessors who worked so hard throughout their lives to rebuild Hiroshima and abolish nuclear weapons. Finally, we appeal to the people of the world: renew your determination. Let us work together with all our might for the abolition of nuclear weapons and the realization of lasting world peace.

＊　＊　＊

---

97) ［名］手を差し伸べること　働きかけ

Peace Declaration (2014)

【Comments by the City of Hiroshima】
〈Including three A-bomb survivors' experiences; indicating that we should put ourselves in the place of the A-bomb survivors, imagine their experiences, communicate, think and act together with them to build a peaceful world without nuclear weapons; pledging to strengthen international public demand for the start of negotiations on a nuclear weapons convention and for promoting measures towards the illegalization of nuclear weapons, focused on their inhumanity; calling on the policymakers of the world to visit the A-bombed cities and apply their resources to a new security system based on trust and dialogue; urging the Japanese government to accept the full weight of the fact that we have avoided war for 69 years thanks to the noble pacifism of the Japanese Constitution, and to continue as a nation of peace in both word and deed〉

Summer, 69 years later. The burning sun takes us back to "that day." August 6, 1945. A single atomic bomb renders Hiroshima a burnt plain. From infants to the elderly, tens of thousands of innocent civilians lose their lives in a single day. By the end of the year, 140,000 have died. To avoid forgetting that sacred sacrifice and to prevent a repetition of that tragedy, please listen to the voices of the survivors.

Approximately 6,000 young boys and girls died

removing buildings for fire lanes. One who was a 12-year-old junior high student at the time says, "Even now, I carry the scars of war and that atomic bombing on my body and in my heart. Nearly all my classmates were killed instantly. My heart is tortured[98] by guilt when I think how badly they wanted to live and that I was the only one who did." Having somehow survived, *hibakusha* still suffer from severe physical and emotional wounds.

"Water, please." Voices from the brink of death are still lodged in the memory of a boy who was 15 and a junior high student. The pleas were from younger students who had been demolishing[99] buildings. Seeing their badly burned, grotesquely swollen faces, eyebrows and eyelashes singed off, school uniforms in ragged[100] tatters due to the heat ray, he tried to respond but was stopped. "'Give water when they're injured that bad and they'll die, boy,' so I closed my ears and refused them water. If I had known they were going to die anyway, I would have given them all the water they wanted." Profound regret persists.

People who rarely talked about the past because of their ghastly experiences are now, in old age, starting to open up. "I want people to know the true cruelty of war," says an A-bomb orphan. He tells of children like himself living in a city of ashes, sleeping under bridges, in the corners of burned-out buildings, in bomb shelters, having nothing more than the clothes on their backs, stealing and fighting to eat, not going to school,

---

98) torture［他動］ひどく苦しめる　さいなませる　99) demolish［他動］破壊する
100)［形］ぼろぼろの

barely surviving day to day working for gangsters.

Immediately after the bombing, a 6-year-old first grader hovered on the border between life and death. Later, she lived a continual fearful struggle with radiation aftereffects. She speaks out now because, "I don't want any young people to go through that experience." After an exchange with non-Japanese war victims, she decided to convey the importance of "young people making friends around the world," and "unceasing efforts to build, not a culture of war, but a culture of peace."

The "absolute evil" that robbed children of loving families and dreams for the future, plunging their lives into turmoil[101], is not susceptible to threats and counterthreats, killing and being killed. Military force just gives rise to new cycles of hatred. To eliminate the evil, we must transcend nationality, race, religion, and other differences, value person-to-person relationships, and build a world that allows forward-looking dialogue.

Hiroshima asks everyone throughout the world to accept this wish of the *hibakusha* and walk with them the path to nuclear weapons abolition and world peace.

Each one of us will help determine the future of the human family. Please put yourself in the place of the *hibakusha*. Imagine their experiences, including that day from the depths of hell, actually happening to you or someone in your family. To make sure the tragedies of Hiroshima and Nagasaki never happen a third time, let's all communicate, think and act together

---

101) [名] 混乱、不安

with the *hibakusha* for a peaceful world without nuclear weapons and without war.

We will do our best. Mayors for Peace, now with over 6,200 member cities, will work through lead cities representing us in their parts of the world and in conjunction with NGOs and the UN to disseminate the facts of the bombings and the message of Hiroshima. We will steadfastly promote the new movement stressing the humanitarian consequences of nuclear weapons and seeking to outlaw them. We will help strengthen international public demand for the start of negotiations on a nuclear weapons convention with the goal of total abolition by 2020.

The Hiroshima Statement that emerged this past April from the ministerial meeting of the NPDI (Non-Proliferation and Disarmament Initiative)[102] called on the world's policymakers to visit Hiroshima and Nagasaki. President Obama and all leaders of nuclear-armed nations, please respond to that call by visiting the A-bombed cities as soon as possible to see what happened with your own eyes. If you do, you will be convinced that nuclear weapons are an absolute evil that must no longer be allowed to exist. Please stop using the inhumane threat of this absolute evil to defend your countries. Rather, apply all your resources to a new security system based on trust and dialogue.

Japan is the only A-bombed nation. Precisely because our security situation is increasingly severe, our government should accept the full weight of the fact

---

102) NPDI (Non-Proliferation and Disarmament Initiative)　軍縮・不拡散イニシアティブ

that we have avoided war for 69 years thanks to the noble pacifism of the Japanese Constitution. We must continue as a nation of peace in both word and deed, working with other countries toward the new security system. Looking toward next year's NPT Review Conference, Japan should bridge the gap between the nuclear-weapon and non-nuclear-weapon states to strengthen the NPT regime. In addition, I ask the government to expand the "black rain areas" and, by providing more caring assistance, show more compassion for the *hibakusha* and all those suffering from the effects of radiation.

Here and now, as we offer our heartfelt consolation to the souls of those sacrificed to the atomic bomb, we pledge to join forces with people the world over seeking the abolition of the absolute evil, nuclear weapons, and the realization of lasting world peace.

* * *

Peace Declaration (2013)

【Comments by the City of Hiroshima】
〈Including five A-bomb survivors' experiences; calling for everyone to act as a momentum in working for nuclear weapons abolition, in response to the wishes of the A-bomb survivors; calling on the policymakers of the world to visit Hiroshima and apply their resources to a new security system based on trust and dialogue;

⟨ calling for the efforts of involved countries to work towards the denuclearization of North Ko-rea and to establish the Northeast Asia nuclear-weapon-free zone; urging the Japanese government to strengthen ties with other countries calling for nuclear abolition, based on the inhumanity of nuclear weapons and to improve its support measures for the A-bomb survivors and for those exposed to the black rain, and expand the black rain areas; calling upon the Japanese government to establish responsible energy initiatives that put top priority on the lives and safety of the people⟩

We greet the morning of the 68th return of "that day." At 8:15 a.m., August 6, 1945, a single atomic bomb erased an entire family. "The baby boy was safely born. Just as the family was celebrating, the atomic bomb exploded. Showing no mercy, it took all that joy and hope along with the new life."

A little boy managed somehow to survive but the atomic bomb took his entire family. This A-bomb orphan lived through hardship, isolation, and illness, but was never able to have a family of his own. Today, he is a lonely old *hibakusha*. "I have never once been glad I survived," he says, looking back. After all these years of terrible suffering, the deep hurt remains.

A woman who experienced the bombing at the age of eight months suffered discrimination and prejudice. She did manage to marry, but a month later, her mother-in-law, who had been so kind at first, learned about her A-bomb survivor's handbook. "'You're a *hibakusha*,' she said, 'We don't need a bombed bride. Get out now.' And with that, I was divorced." At times, the fear of radiation elicited ugliness and cruelty. Groundless rumors caused many survivors to suffer in marriage, employment, childbirth—at every stage of life.

Indiscriminately stealing the lives of innocent people, permanently altering the lives of survivors, and stalking their minds and bodies to the end of their days, the atomic bomb is the ultimate inhumane weapon and an absolute evil. The *hibakusha*, who know the hell of an atomic bombing, have continuously fought that evil.

Under harsh, painful circumstances, the *hibakusha* have struggled with anger, hatred, grief and other agonizing emotions. Suffering with aftereffects, over and over they cried, "I want to be healthy. Can't I just lead a normal life?" But precisely because they had suffered such tragedy themselves, they came to believe that no one else "should ever have to experience this cruelty." A man who was 14 at the time of the bombing pleads, "If the people of the world could just share love for the Earth and love for all people, an end to war would be more than a dream."

Even as their average age surpasses 78, the *hibakusha* continue to communicate their longing for peace. They still hope the people of the world will come to share that longing and choose the right path. In response to this desire of the many *hibakusha* who have transcended such terrible pain and sorrow, the rest of us must become the force that drives the struggle to abolish nuclear weapons.

To that end, the city of Hiroshima and the more than 5,700 cities that comprise Mayors for Peace, in collaboration with the UN and like-minded NGOs, seek to abolish nuclear weapons by 2020 and throw our full weight behind the early achievement of a nuclear weapons convention.

Policymakers of the world, how long will you remain imprisoned by distrust and animosity? Do you honestly believe you can continue to maintain national security by rattling your sabers[103]? Please come to Hiroshima. Encounter the spirit of the *hibakusha*. Look squarely at the future of the human family without being trapped in the past, and make the decision to shift to a system of security based on trust and dialogue. Hiroshima is a place that embodies[104] the grand pacifism of the Japanese constitution. At the same time, it points to the path the human family must walk. Moreover, for the peace and stability of our region, all countries involved must do more to achieve a nuclear-weapon-free North Korea in a Northeast Asia nuclear-weapon-free zone.

Today, a growing group of countries is focusing on the humanitarian consequences of nuclear weapons and calling for abolition. President Obama has demonstrated his commitment to nuclear disarmament by inviting Russia to start negotiating further reductions. In this context, even if the nuclear power

---

103) rattle one's saber サーベルをガタガタ鳴らす、武力をちらつかせて脅す
104) embody［他動］具体化する

agreement the Japanese government is negotiating with India promotes their economic relationship, it is likely to hinder nuclear weapons abolition. Hiroshima calls on the Japanese government to strengthen ties with the governments pursuing abolition. At the ministerial meeting of the Non-Proliferation and Disarmament Initiative next spring in Hiroshima, we hope Japan will lead the way toward a stronger NPT regime. And, as the *hibakusha* in Japan and overseas advance in age, we reiterate[105] our demand for improved measures appropriate to their needs. As well, we demand measures for those exposed to the black rain and an expansion of the "black rain areas."

This summer, eastern Japan is still suffering the aftermath[106] of the great earthquake and the nuclear accident. The desperate struggle to recover hometowns continues. The people of Hiroshima know well the ordeal of recovery. We extend our hearts to all those affected and will continue to offer our support. We urge the national government to rapidly develop and implement a responsible energy policy that places top priority on safety and the livelihoods of the people.

Recalling once again the trials of our predecessors through these 68 years, we offer heartfelt consolation to the souls of the atomic bomb victims by pledging to do everything in our power to eliminate the absolute evil of nuclear weapons and achieve a peaceful world.

*　　*　　*

105) reiterate［他動］繰り返して言う　106)［名］影響、余波

Peace Declaration (2012)

【Comments by the City of Hiroshima】
〈Including three A-bomb survivors' experiences; introducing the fact that the city has begun training official *hibakusha* successors; calling on policymakers from nuclear-armed nations to visit Hiroshima in order to think about peace; calling on the Japanese government to take leadership towards nuclear weapons abolition; touching upon the fact that the experiences of the sufferers from the Great East Japan Earthquake disaster and nuclear accident overlap with those of the A-bomb survivors, and that our hearts are with them; urging the Japanese government to quickly establish energy measures to protect the lives and safety of the citizens, and to make the political decision to expand the black rain areas〉

8:15 a.m., August 6, 1945. Our hometown was reduced to ashes by a single atomic bomb. The houses we came home to, our everyday lives, the customs we cherished[107]—all were gone: "Hiroshima was no more. The city had vanished. No roads, just a burnt plain of rubble[108] as far as I could see, and sadly, I could see too far. I followed electric lines that had fallen along what I took to be tram rails. The tram street was hot. Death was all around." That was our city, as seen by a young woman of twenty. That was Hiroshima for all the survivors. The exciting festivals, the playing in boats,

---

107) cherish［他動］大切にする　108) ［名］がれき

the fishing and clamming[109], the children catching long-armed shrimp—a way of life had disappeared from our beloved rivers.

Worse yet, the bomb snuffed out the sacred lives of so many human beings: "I rode in a truck with a civil defense team to pick up corpses. I was just a boy, so they told me to grab the ankles. I did, but the skin slipped right off. I couldn't hold on. I steeled myself[110], squeezed hard with my fingertips, and the flesh started oozing[111]. A terrible stench. I gripped right down to the bone. With a 'one-two-three,' we tossed them into the truck." As seen in the experience of this 13-year-old boy, our city had become a living hell. Countless corpses lay everywhere, piled on top of each other; amid the moans of unearthly[112] voices, infants sucked at the breasts of dead mothers, while dazed, empty-eyed mothers clutched their dead babies.

A girl of sixteen lost her whole family, one after the other: "My 7-year-old brother was burned from head to toe. He died soon after the bombing. A month later, my parents died; then, my 13-year-old brother and my 11-year-old sister. The only ones left were myself and my little brother, who was three, and he died later of cancer." From newborns to grandmothers, by the end of the year, 140,000 precious lives were taken from Hiroshima.

Hiroshima was plunged into deepest darkness. Our *hibakusha* experienced the bombing in flesh and blood. Then, they had to live with aftereffects and social

---

109) clam [自動] 貝採りをする 110) steel oneself 心を鬼にする、覚悟を決める
111) ooze [自動] じくじく流れ出る 112) [形] 恐ろしい

prejudice. Even so, they soon began telling the world about their experience. Transcending rage and hatred, they revealed the utter inhumanity of nuclear weapons and worked tirelessly to abolish those weapons. We want the whole world to know of their hardship, their grief, their pain, and their selfless desire.

The average *hibakusha* is now over 78. This summer, in response to the many ordinary citizens seeking to inherit and pass on their experience and desire, Hiroshima has begun carefully training official *hibakusha* successors. Determined never to let the atomic bombing fade from memory, we intend to share with ever more people at home and abroad the *hibakusha* desire for a nuclear-weapon-free world.

People of the world! Especially leaders of nuclear-armed nations, please come to Hiroshima to contemplate peace in this A-bombed city.

This year, Mayors for Peace marked its 30th anniversary. The number of cities calling for the total abolition of nuclear weapons by 2020 has passed 5,300, and our members now represent approximately a billion people. Next August, we will hold a Mayors for Peace general conference in Hiroshima. That event will convey to the world the intense desire of the overwhelming majority of our citizens for a nuclear weapons convention and elimination of nuclear weapons. The following spring, Hiroshima will host a ministerial meeting of the Non-Proliferation and Disarmament Initiative comprising ten non-nuclear-weapon states, including Japan. I firmly believe that the demand for freedom from nuclear weapons will soon spread out from Hiroshima, encircle the globe, and lead us to genuine world peace.

March 11, 2011, is a day we will never forget. A natural disaster compounded by a nuclear power accident created an unprecedented catastrophe[113]. Here in Hiroshima, we are keenly aware that the survivors of that catastrophe still suffer terribly, yet look toward the future with hope. We see their ordeal clearly superimposed on what we endured 67 years ago. I speak now to all in the stricken areas. Please hold fast to your hope for tomorrow. Your day will arrive, absolutely. Our hearts are with you.

Having learned a lesson from that horrific accident, Japan is now engaged in a national debate over its energy policy, with some voices insisting, "Nuclear energy and humankind cannot coexist." I call on the Japanese government to establish without delay an energy policy that guards the safety and security of the people. I ask the government of the only country to experience an atomic bombing to accept as its own the resolve of Hiroshima and Nagasaki. Mindful of the unstable situation surrounding us in Northeast Asia, please display bolder leadership in the movement to eliminate nuclear weapons. Please also provide more caring measures for the *hibakusha* in and out of Japan who still suffer even today, and take the political decision to expand the "black rain areas."

---

113) [名]大惨事

Once again, we offer our heartfelt prayers for the peaceful repose of the atomic bomb victims. From our base here in Hiroshima, we pledge to convey to the world the experience and desire of our *hibakusha*, and do everything in our power to achieve the genuine peace of a world without nuclear weapons.

*   *   *

Peace Declaration (2011)

【Comments by the City of Hiroshima】
〈Incorporating two A-bomb survivors' experiences; expressing our determination to learn from all the *hibakusha* what they experienced and their desire for peace, and communicating what we learn to future generations and the rest of the world; announcing our commitment to expand Mayors for Peace; urging all countries, especially the nuclear-armed states, including the United States of America, which continues its subcritical nuclear testing and related experiments, to pursue enthusiastically a process that will abolish nuclear weapons; announcing that we will strive to host an international conference to discuss the nuclear non-proliferation regime; urging the Japanese government to quickly review our energy policies and institute concrete countermeasures, referring to the Great East Japan Earthquake and the accident at Tokyo Electric Power Company's Fukushima Daiichi Nuclear Power

Station⟩

Sixty-six years ago, despite the war, the people of Hiroshima were leading fairly normal lives. Until that fateful moment, many families were enjoying life together right here in what is now Peace Memorial Park and was then one of the city's most prosperous districts. A man who was thirteen at the time shares this: "August fifth was a Sunday, and for me, a second-year student in middle school, the first full day off in a very long time. I asked a good friend from school to come with me, and we went on down to the river. Forgetting all about the time, we stayed until twilight, swimming and playing on the sandy riverbed. That hot mid-summer's day was the last time I ever saw him."

The next morning, August sixth at 8:15, a single atomic bomb ripped those normal lives out by the roots. This description is from a woman who was sixteen at the time: "My forty-kilogram body was blown seven meters by the blast, and I was knocked out. When I came to, it was pitch black and utterly silent. In that soundless world, I thought I was the only one left. I was naked except for some rags around my hips. The skin on my left arm had peeled off[114] in five-centimeter strips that were all curled up[115]. My right arm was sort of whitish. Putting my hands to my face, I found my right cheek quite rough while my left cheek was all slimy."

Their community and lives ravaged by an atomic bomb, the survivors were stunned and injured, and yet,

---

114) peel off はがす   115) curl up 巻きあがる

they did their best to help each other: "Suddenly, I heard lots of voices crying and screaming, 'Help!' 'Mommy, help!' Turning to a voice nearby I said, 'I'll help you.' I tried to move in that direction but my body was so heavy. I did manage to move enough to save one young child, but with no skin on my hands, I was unable to help any more. …'I'm really sorry.' …"

Such scenes were unfolding not just here where this park is but all over Hiroshima. Wanting to help but unable to do so—many also still live with the guilt of being their family's sole survivor.

Based on their own experiences and carrying in their hearts the voices and feelings of those sacrificed to the bomb, the *hibakusha* called for a world without nuclear weapons as they struggled day by day to survive. In time, along with other Hiroshima residents, and with generous assistance from Japan and around the world, they managed to bring their city back to life.

Their average age is now over 77. Calling forth what remains of the strength that revived their city, they continue to pursue the lasting peace of a world free from nuclear weapons. Can we let it go at this? Absolutely not. The time has come for the rest of us to learn from all the *hibakusha* what they experienced and their desire for peace. Then, we must communicate what we learn to future generations and the rest of the world.

Through this Peace Declaration, I would like to communicate the *hibakusha* experience and desire for peace to each and every person on this planet. Hiroshima will pour everything we have into working, along with Nagasaki, to expand Mayors for Peace such that all cities, those places around the world where people gather, will strive together to eliminate nuclear weapons by 2020. Moreover, we want all countries, especially the nuclear-armed states, including the United States of America, which continues its subcritical nuclear testing[116] and related experiments, to pursue enthusiastically a process that will abolish nuclear weapons. To that end, we plan to host an international conference that will bring the world's policymakers to Hiroshima to discuss the nuclear non-proliferation regime.[117]

The Great East Japan Earthquake of March eleventh this year was so destructive it revived images of Hiroshima 66 years ago and still pains our hearts. Here in Hiroshima we sincerely pray for the souls of all who perished and strongly support the survivors, wishing them the quickest possible recovery.

The accident at Tokyo Electric Power Company's Fukushima Daiichi Nuclear Power Station and the ongoing threat of radiation have generated tremendous anxiety among those in the affected areas and many others. The trust the Japanese people once had in nuclear power has been shattered. From the common admonition[118] that "nuclear energy and humankind cannot coexist," some seek to abandon nuclear power altogether. Others advocate extremely strict control of

---

116) subcritical nuclear testing 臨界前核実験   117) non-proliferation regime 核不拡散体制   118) [名]訓戒

nuclear power and increased utilization of renewable energy.

The Japanese government should humbly accept this reality, quickly review our energy policies, and institute concrete countermeasures to regain the understanding and trust of the people. In addition, with our *hibakusha* aging, we demand that the Japanese government promptly expand its "black rain areas" and offer more comprehensive and caring assistance measures to all *hibakusha* regardless of their countries of residence.

Offering our heartfelt condolences to the souls of the A-bomb victims, reaffirming our conviction that "the atomic bombing must never be repeated" and "no one else should ever have to suffer like this," we hereby pledge to do everything in our power to abolish nuclear weapons and build lasting world peace.

CHAPTER 2

TADATOSHI AKIBA's [1]
PEACE DECLARATION

(2010–1999)

Peace Declaration (2010)

【Comments by the City of Hiroshima】

〈Asserting that the *hibakusha*'s message that "no one else should ever suffer as we did" is a beacon to the world; pointing out that the Final Document passed at the NPT Review Conference this year confirms that our future depends on the steps articulated by Hiroshima, Nagasaki, and Mayors for Peace; stating that through the voice of civil society and the leadership of UN Secretary General Ban Ki-Moon and President Obama, this year's NPT Review Conference was a success; calling upon the Japanese prime minister to commit himself to the *hibakusha*'s dreams of a nuclear-weapon-free world and demonstrate his leadership; announcing that we will follow the Hiroshima Appeal adopted at the Hiroshima Conference for the Total Abolition for Nuclear Weapons by 2020〉

In the company of *hibakusha* who, on this day 65 years ago, were hurled, without understanding why, into a "hell" beyond their most terrifying nightmares and yet somehow managed to survive; together with the many souls that fell victim to unwarranted[2] death, we greet this August sixth with re-energized determination that, "No one else should ever have to suffer such horror."

Through the unwavering[3] will of the *hibakusha* and other residents, with help from around Japan and the world, Hiroshima is now recognized as a beautiful city. Today, we aspire to be a "model city for the world" and even to host the Olympic Games. Transcending the tortures[4] of hell, trusting in the peace-loving peoples of the world, the *hibakusha* offer a message that is the cornerstone of Japan's Peace Constitution and a beacon[5] to the world.

The results of the NPT Review Conference held this past May testify to that beacon's guiding influence. The Final Document expresses the unanimous intent of the parties to seek the abolition of nuclear weapons; notes the valuable contribution of civil society; notes that a majority favors the establishment of timelines for the nuclear weapons abolition process, and highlights the need for a nuclear weapons convention or new legal framework. In doing so, it confirms that our future depends on taking the steps articulated by Hiroshima, Nagasaki, the more than 4,000 city members of Mayors for Peace, and the two-thirds of all Japanese municipalities that formally supported the Hiroshima-Nagasaki Protocol[6].

---

2) ［形］不当な　※ unwarranted death 非業の死　3) ［形］確固とした
4) ［名］拷問、激しい苦痛　5) ［名］かがり火、灯台　6) ［名］議定書

That our cry of conscience, the voice of civil society yearning for a future free from nuclear weapons, was heard at the UN is due in large measure to the leadership of His Excellency Ban Ki-moon, who today has become the first UN Secretary-General to attend our Peace Memorial Ceremony. President Obama, the United States government, and the 1,200-member U.S. Conference of Mayors[7] also wielded their powerful influence.

This ceremony is honored today by the presence of government officials representing more than 70 countries as well as the representatives of many international organizations, NGOs, and citizens' groups. These guests have come to join the *hibakusha*, their families, and the people of Hiroshima in sharing grief and prayers for a peaceful world. Nuclear-weapon states Russia, China and others have attended previously, but today, for the first time ever, we have with us the U.S. ambassador and officials from the UK and France.

Clearly, the urgency of nuclear weapons abolition is permeating[8] our global conscience; the voice of the vast majority is becoming the preeminent[9] force for change in the international community.

To seize this unprecedented opportunity and actually achieve a world without nuclear weapons, we need above all to communicate to every corner of our planet the intense yearning of the *hibakusha*, thereby narrowing the gap between their passion and the rest of

---

7) U.S. Conference of Mayors 全米市長会議　8) permeate［他動］浸透する
9)［形］傑出した、卓越した

the world. Unfortunately, many are unaware of the urgency; their eyes still closed to the fact that only through luck, not wisdom, have we avoided human extinction.

Now the time is ripe for the Japanese government to take decisive action. It should begin to "take the lead in the pursuit of the elimination of nuclear weapons" by legislating into law the three non-nuclear principles[10], abandoning the U.S. nuclear umbrella, legally recognizing the expanded "black rain areas," and implementing compassionate, caring assistance measures for all the aging *hibakusha* anywhere in the world.

In addition, the Prime Minister's wholehearted commitment and action to make the dreams of the *hibakusha* come true would lead us all by 2020 to a new world of "zero nuclear weapons," an achievement that would rival in human history the "discovery of zero" itself. He could, for example, confront the leaders of the nuclear-weapon states with the urgent need for abolition, lead them to the table to sign a nuclear weapons convention, and call on all countries for sharp reductions in nuclear and other military expenditures. His options are infinite.

We citizens and cities will act as well. In accordance with the Hiroshima Appeal adopted during last week's Hiroshima Conference for the Total Abolition of Nuclear Weapons by 2020, we will work closely with like-minded nations, NGOs, and the UN itself to

---

10) three non-nuclear principles 非核三原則 ※ non-possession, non-production, and non-introduction of nuclear weapons

generate an ever-larger tidal wave of demand for a world free of nuclear weapons by 2020.

Finally, on this, the 65th anniversary of the atomic bombing, as we offer to the souls of the A-bomb victims our heartfelt condolences, we hereby declare that we cannot force the most patiently enduring people in the world, the *hibakusha*, to be patient any longer. Now is the time to devote ourselves unreservedly to the most crucial duty facing the human family, to give the *hibakusha*, within their lifetimes, the nuclear-weapon-free world that will make them blissfully exclaim, "I'm so happy I lived to see this day."

*   *   *

Peace Declaration (2009)

【Comments by the City of Hiroshima】
⟨Pointing out that the *hibakusha* who are still suffering have been granted legal support through the courageous court decision accepting the fact that the effects of radiation on the human body have yet to be fully elucidated; Suggesting that we refer to ourselves as the "Obamajority," the great global majority that supports the abolition of nuclear weapons; stating that global democracy that respects the majority will of the world and solves problems through the power of the people has truly begun to grow; proposing the creation of a "Lower House" of the UN to deliver the voices of the

people directly to the UN; calling on the world's citizens to come together and fully strive to eliminate nuclear weapons⟩

That weapon of human extinction, the atomic bomb, was dropped on the people of Hiroshima sixty-four years ago. Yet the *hibakusha's* suffering, a hell no words can convey, continues. Radiation absorbed 64 years earlier continues to eat at their bodies, and memories of 64 years ago flash back as if they had happened yesterday.

Fortunately, the grave implications[11] of the *hibakusha* experience are granted legal support. A good example of this support is the courageous court decision humbly accepting the fact that the effects of radiation on the human body have yet to be fully elucidated[12]. The Japanese national government should make its assistance measures fully appropriate to the situations of the aging *hibakusha*, including those exposed in "black rain areas" and those living overseas. Then, tearing down the walls between its ministries and agencies, it should lead the world as standard-bearer for the movement to abolish nuclear weapons by 2020 to actualize the fervent desire of *hibakusha* that "No one else should ever suffer as we did."

In April this year, US President Obama speaking in Prague said, "...as the only nuclear power to have used a nuclear weapon, the United States has a moral responsibility to act." And "...take concrete steps

---

11) ［名］結果　12) elucidate［他動］はっきりさせる

towards a world without nuclear weapons." Nuclear weapons abolition is the will not only of the *hibaku-sha* but also of the vast majority of people and nations on this planet. The fact that President Obama is listening to those voices has solidified our conviction that "the only role for nuclear weapons is to be abolished."

In response, we support President Obama and have a moral responsibility to act to abolish nuclear weapons. To emphasize this point, we refer to ourselves, the great global majority, as the "Obamajority[13]," and we call on the rest of the world to join forces with us to eliminate all nuclear weapons by 2020. The essence of this idea is embodied in the Japanese Constitution, which is ever more highly esteemed around the world.

Now, with more than 3,000 member cities worldwide, Mayors for Peace has given concrete substance to our "2020 Vision" through the Hiroshima-Nagasaki Protocol, and we are doing everything in our power to promote its adoption at the NPT Review Conference next year. Once the Protocol is adopted, our scenario calls for an immediate halt to all efforts to acquire or deploy nuclear weapons by all countries, including the Democratic People's Republic of Korea, which has so recently conducted defiant nuclear tests; visits by leaders of nuclear-weapon states and suspect states to the A-bombed cities; early convening of a UN Special Session devoted to Disarmament; an immediate start to negotiations with the goal of concluding a nuclear

---

13) 秋葉忠利氏の造語で「核なき世界」を提唱したオバマ米大統領を支持する国際社会の多数派を指す

weapons convention by 2015; and finally, to eliminate all nuclear weapons by 2020. We will adopt a more detailed plan at the Mayors for Peace General Conference that begins tomorrow in Nagasaki.

The year 2020 is important because we wish to enter a world without nuclear weapons with as many *hibakusha* as possible. Furthermore, if our generation fails to eliminate nuclear weapons, we will have failed to fulfill our minimum responsibility to those that follow.

Global Zero, the International Commission on Nuclear Non-proliferation and Disarmament[14] and others of influence throughout the world have initiated positive programs that seek the abolition of nuclear weapons. We sincerely hope that they will all join the circle of those pressing for 2020.

As seen in the anti-personnel landmine ban, liberation from poverty through the Grameen Bank, the prevention of global warming and other such movements, global democracy that respects the majority will of the world and solves problems through the power of the people has truly begun to grow. To nurture this growth and go on to solve other major problems, we must create a mechanism by which the voices of the people can be delivered directly into the UN. One idea would be to create a "Lower House" of the United Nations made up of 100 cities that have suffered major tragedies due to war and other disasters, plus another 100 cities with large populations, totaling 200 cities. The current UN General Assembly would

---

14) International Commission on Nuclear Non-proliferation and Disarmament 核不拡散・核軍縮に関する国際委員会

then become the "Upper House."

On the occasion of the Peace Memorial Ceremony commemorating the 64th anniversary of the atomic bombing, we offer our solemn, heartfelt condolence to the souls of the A-bomb victims, and, together with the city of Nagasaki and the majority of Earth's people and nations, we pledge to strive with all our strength for a world free from nuclear weapons.

We have the power. We have the responsibility. And we are the Obamajority. Together, we can abolish nuclear weapons. Yes, we can.

*   *   *

Peace Declaration (2008)

【Comments by the City of Hiroshima】
〈Asserting the truth that the only role for nuclear weapons is to be abolished; indicating that the majority of world citizens seek nuclear weapons abolition; expressing expectation that the new president of the United States will listen to the majority, for whom human survival is the top priority; announcing that Mayors for Peace proposed the Hiroshi-ma-Nagasaki Protocol to realize a world without nuclear weapons by 2020; indicating the importance of a "paradigm shift" toward modeling the world on intercity relationships built on mutual understanding and trust; expressing the hope that the G8 Speakers' Meeting in Hiroshima will

〈help spread the *hibakusha* philosophy around the world〉

Another August 6, and the horrors of 63 years ago arise undiminished in the minds of our *hibakusha*, whose average age now exceeds 75. "Water, please!" "Help me!" "Mommy!" — On this day, we, too, etch in our hearts the voices, faces and forms that vanished in the hell no *hibakusha* can ever forget, renewing our determination that "No one else should ever suffer as we did."

Because the effects of that atomic bomb, still eating away at the minds and bodies of the *hibakusha*, have for decades been so underestimated, a complete picture of the damage has yet to emerge. Most severely neglected have been the emotional injuries. Therefore, the city of Hiroshima is initiating a two-year scientific exploration of the psychological impact of the A-bomb experience.

This study should teach us the grave import of the truth, born of tragedy and suffering, that "the only role for nuclear weapons is to be abolished."

This truth received strong support from a report compiled last November by the city of Hiroshima. Scientists and other nuclear-related experts exploring the damage from a postulated[15] nuclear attack found once again that only way to protect citizens from such an attack is the total abolition of nuclear weapons. This is precisely why the Nuclear Non-Proliferation Treaty and the International Court of Justice[16] advisory[17]

15) postulate [他動] 想定する　16) International Court of Justice 国際司法裁判所　17) [形] 勧告的な、助言的な [名] 勧告、忠告

opinion state clearly that all nations are obligated to engage in good-faith negotiations leading to complete nuclear disarmament. Furthermore, even leaders previously central to creating and implementing US nuclear policy are now repeatedly demanding a world without nuclear weapons.

We who seek the abolition of nuclear weapons are the majority. United Cities and Local Governments, which represents the majority of the Earth's population, has endorsed the Mayors for Peace campaign. One hundred ninety states have ratified the Nuclear Non-Proliferation Treaty. One hundred thirteen countries and regions have signed nuclear-weapon-free zone treaties. Last year, 170 countries voted in favor of Japan's UN resolution calling for the abolition of nuclear weapons. Only three countries, the US among them, opposed this resolution. We can only hope that the president of the United States elected this November will listen conscientiously to the majority, for whom the top priority is human survival.

To achieve the will of the majority by 2020, Mayors for Peace, now with 2,368 city members worldwide, proposed in April of this year a Hiroshima-Nagasaki Protocol to supplement the Nuclear Non-Proliferation Treaty. This Protocol calls for an immediate halt to all efforts, including by nuclear-weapon states, to obtain or deploy nuclear weapons, with a legal ban on all acquisition[18] or use to follow by 2015. Thus, it draws a concrete road map to a nuclear-weapon-free world.

---

18) [名]獲得

Now, with our destination and the map to that destination clear, all we need is the strong will and capacity to act to guard the future for our children.

World citizens and like-minded nations have achieved treaties banning anti-personnel landmines and cluster munitions[19]. Meanwhile, the most effective measures against global warming are coming from cities. Citizens cooperating at the city level can solve the problems of the human family because cities are home to the majority of the world's population, cities do not have militaries, and cities have built genuine partnerships around the world based on mutual understanding and trust.

The Japanese Constitution is an appropriate point of departure for a "paradigm shift[20]" toward modeling the world on intercity relationships. I hereby call on the Japanese government to fiercely defend our Constitution, press all governments to adopt the Hiroshima-Nagasaki Protocol, and play a leading role in the effort to abolish nuclear weapons. I further request greater generosity in designating A-bomb illnesses and in relief measures appropriate to the current situations of our aging *hibakusha*, including those exposed in "black rain areas" and those living overseas.

Next month the G8 Speakers' Meeting will, for the first time, take place in Japan. I fervently hope that Hiroshima's hosting of this meeting will help our "*hibakusha* philosophy" spread throughout the world.

Now, on the occasion of this 63rd anniversary Peace

19) cluster munitions クラスター弾　20) paradigm shift　パラダイムシフト、パラダイム転換

Memorial Ceremony, we offer our heartfelt lamentations[21] for the souls of the atomic bomb victims and, in concert with the city of Nagasaki and with citizens around the world, pledge to do everything in our power to accomplish the total eradication of nuclear weapons.

*   *   *

Peace Declaration (2007)

【Comments by the City of Hiroshima】
〈Expressing the importance of the message that was born from the suffering of the *hibakusha*; insisting that we must never forget their accomplishments in preventing a third use of nuclear weapons by speaking of experiences they would rather forget; indicating that because of a handful of old-fashioned leaders, clinging to an early 20th century worldview in thrall to the rule of brute strength, the human family faced the peril of extinction, recognizing the 21st century as a time in which our problems can actually be solved through the power of the people, calling attention to examples of human wisdom, which has led to democratic governments and international rules, giving cities across the world the ability to rise up with their citizens to leverage their voices to lift international politics; pledging to take all actions required to bequeath to future generations a nuclear-weapon-free world〉

---

21) ［名］嘆き悲しむこと

That fateful summer, 8:15. The roar of a B-29 breaks the morning calm. A parachute opens in the blue sky. Then suddenly, a flash, an enormous blast—silence—hell on Earth.

The eyes of young girls watching the parachute were melted. Their faces became giant charred blisters[22]. The skin of people seeking help dangled from their fingernails. Their hair stood on end. Their clothes were ripped to shreds. People trapped in houses toppled by the blast were burned alive. Others died when their eyeballs and internal organs burst from their bodies—Hiroshima was a hell where those who somehow survived envied the dead.

Within the year, 140,000 had died. Many who escaped death initially are still suffering from leukemia[23], thyroid cancer[24], and a vast array of other afflictions[25].

But there was more. Sneered at for their keloid scars, discriminated against in employment and marriage, unable to find understanding for profound emotional wounds, survivors suffered and struggled day after day, questioning the meaning of life.

And yet, the message born of that agony is a beam of light now shining the way for the human family. To ensure that "no one else ever suffers as we did," the *hibakusha* have continuously spoken of experiences they would rather forget, and we must never forget their accomplishments in preventing a third use of nuclear weapons.

Despite their best efforts, vast arsenals of nuclear

---

22) [名]火ぶくれ　23) [名]白血病　24) thyroid cancer 甲状腺がん
25) [名]苦痛

weapons remain in high states of readiness—deployed or easily available. Proliferation is gaining momentum, and the human family still faces the peril of extinction. This is because a handful of old-fashioned leaders, clinging to an early 20th century worldview in thrall to the rule of brute[26] strength, are rejecting global democracy, turning their backs on the reality of the atomic bombings and the message of the *hibakusha*.

However, here in the 21st century the time has come when these problems can actually be solved through the power of the people. Former colonies have become independent. Democratic governments have taken root. Learning the lessons of history, people have created international rules prohibiting attacks on non-combatants and the use of inhumane weapons. They have worked hard to make the United Nations an instrument for the resolution of international disputes. And now city governments, entities that have always walked with and shared in the tragedy and pain of their citizens, are rising up. In the light of human wisdom, they are leveraging the voices of their citizens to lift international politics.

Because "Cities suffer most from war," Mayors for Peace, with 1,698 city members around the world, is actively campaigning to eliminate all nuclear weapons by 2020.

In Hiroshima, we are continuing our effort to communicate the A-bomb experience by holding A-bomb exhibitions in 101 cities in the US and

---

26) [名]けだもの

facilitating establishment of *Hiroshima-Nagasaki Peace Study Courses* in universities around the world. American mayors have taken the lead in our *Cities Are Not Targets* project. Mayors in the Czech Republic are opposing the deployment of a missile defense system. The mayor of Guernica-Lumo is calling for a resurgence[27] of morality in international politics. The mayor of Ypres is providing an international secretariat for Mayors for Peace, while other Belgian mayors are contributing funds, and many more mayors around the world are working with their citizens on pioneering initiatives. In October this year, at the World Congress of United Cities and Local Governments, which represents the majority of our planet's population, cities will express the will of humanity as we call for the elimination of nuclear weapons.

The government of Japan, the world's only A-bombed nation, is duty-bound to humbly learn the philosophy of the *hibakusha* along with the facts of the atomic bombings and to spread this knowledge through the world. At the same time, to abide by[28] international law and fulfill its good-faith obligation to press for nuclear weapons abolition, the Japanese government should take pride in and protect, as is, the Peace Constitution, while clearly saying "No," to obsolete[29] and mistaken US policies. We further demand, on behalf of the *hibakusha* whose average age now exceeds 74, improved and appropriate assistance, to be extended also to those living overseas or exposed in "black rain

---

27)［名］復活　28) abide by~ 〜に従う、〜を順守する　29)［形］時代遅れの

areas."

Sixty-two years after the atomic bombing, we offer today our heartfelt prayers for the peaceful repose of all its victims and of Iccho Itoh[30], the mayor of Nagasaki shot down on his way toward nuclear weapons abolition. Let us pledge here and now to take all actions required to bequeath to future generations a nuclear-weapon-free world.

*   *   *

Peace Declaration (2006)

【Comments by the City of Hiroshima】
⟨Indicating that obligations for nuclear disarmament are not being upheld despite 10 years having passed since the International Court of Justice handed down an advisory opinion that "...the threat or use of nuclear weapons would generally be contrary to the rules of international law"; announcing the Good Faith Challenge, a campaign to promote the good-faith negotiations for nuclear disarmament, and the Cities Are Not Targets (CANT) project demanding that nuclear-weapon states stop targeting cities for nuclear attack⟩

Radiation, heat, blast and their synergetic effects created a hell on Earth. Sixty-one years later, the number of nations enamored of [31]evil and enslaved by

---

30) 伊藤一長 (元長崎市長)   31) enamored of ~ ～のとりこになっている

nuclear weapons is increasing. The human family stands at a crossroads. Will all nations be enslaved? Or will all nations be liberated? This choice poses another question. Is it acceptable for cities, and especially the innocent children who live in them, to be targeted by nuclear weapons?

The answer is crystal clear, and the past sixty-one years have shown us the path to liberation.

From a hell in which no one could have blamed them for choosing death, the *hibakusha* set forth toward life and the future. Living with injuries and illnesses eating away at body and mind, they have spoken persistently about their experiences. Refusing to bow before discrimination, slander[32], and scorn[33], they have warned continuously that "no one else should ever suffer as we did." Their voices, picked up by people of conscience the world over, are becoming a powerful mass chorus.

The keynote is, "The only role for nuclear weapons is to be abolished." And yet, the world's political leaders continue to ignore these voices. The International Court of Justice advisory opinion handed down ten years ago, born of the creative action of global civil society, should have been a highly effective tool for enlightening[34] and guiding them toward the truth.

The Court found that "...the threat or use of nuclear weapons would generally be contrary to the rules of international law," and went on to declare, "There exists an obligation to pursue in good faith and bring to a

---

32) [名]中傷 33) [名]軽蔑 34) enlighten[他動]教え導く

conclusion negotiations leading to nuclear disarmament in all its aspects under strict and effective international control."

If the nuclear-weapon states had taken the lead and sought in good faith to fulfill this obligation, nuclear weapons would have been abolished already. Unfortunately, during the past ten years, most nations and most people have failed to confront this obligation head-on. Regretting that we have not done more, the City of Hiroshima, along with Mayors for Peace, whose member cities have increased to 1,403, is launching Phase II of our *2020 Vision Campaign*. This phase includes the *Good Faith Challenge*[35], a campaign to promote the good-faith negotiations for nuclear disarmament called for in the ICJ advisory opinion, and a *Cities Are Not Targets* project demanding that nuclear-weapon states stop targeting cities for nuclear attack.

Nuclear weapons are illegal, immoral weapons designed to obliterate cities. Our goals are to reveal the delusions[36] behind "nuclear deterrence theory" and the "nuclear umbrella," which hold cities hostage, and to protect, from a legal and moral standpoint, our citizens' right to life.

Taking the lead in this effort is the US Conference of Mayors, representing 1,139 American cities. At its national meeting this past June, the USCM adopted a resolution demanding that all nuclear-weapon states, including the United States, immediately cease all

---

35) Good Faith Challenge　誠実な交渉義務　36) [名]虚妄

targeting of cities with nuclear weapons.

Cities and citizens of the world have a duty to release the lost sheep from the spell and liberate the world from nuclear weapons. The time has come for all of us to awaken and arise with a will that can penetrate rock and a passion that burns like fire.

I call on the Japanese government to advocate for the *hibakusha* and all citizens by conducting a global campaign that will forcefully insist that the nuclear-weapon states "negotiate in good faith for nuclear disarmament." To that end, I demand that the government respect the Peace Constitution of which we should be proud. I further request more generous, people-oriented assistance appropriate to the actual situations of the aging *hibakusha*, including those living overseas and those exposed in "black rain areas."

To console the many victims whose names remain unknown, this year for the first time we added the words, "Many Unknown" to the ledger of victims' names placed in the cenotaph[37]. We humbly pray for the peaceful repose of the souls of all atomic bomb victims and a future of peace and harmony for the human family.

*   *   *

---

37) [名]慰霊碑

Peace Declaration (2005)

【Comments by the City of Hiroshima】
〈Expressing a need to establish an axiom of "Thou shalt not kill" especially, "Thou shalt not kill children," as the highest priority of the human race; designating the period until August 9, 2006 as a year of inheritance, of awakening, and of commitment, and announced the development of various projects for nuclear-weapons abolition; proposing that the First Committee of the UN General Assembly establish a special committee to deliberate and plan for the achievement and maintenance of a nuclear-weapon-free world〉

This August 6, the 60th anniversary of the atomic bombing, is a moment of shared lamentation in which more than 300 thousand souls of A-bomb victims and those who remain behind transcend the boundary between life and death to remember that day. It is also a time of inheritance[38], of awakening, and of commitment, in which we inherit the commitment of the *hibakusha* to the abolition of nuclear weapons and realization of genuine world peace, awaken to our individual responsibilities, and recommit ourselves to take action. This new commitment, building on the desires of all war victims and the millions around the world who are sharing this moment, is creating a harmony that is enveloping our planet.

The keynote of this harmony is the *hibakusha* warning,

---

38) [名]継承

"No one else should ever suffer as we did," along with the cornerstone of all religions and bodies of law, "Thou shalt not kill.[39]" Our sacred obligation to future generations is to establish this axiom[40], especially its corollary[41], "Thou shalt not kill children," as the highest priority for the human race across all nations and religions. The International Court of Justice advisory opinion issued nine years ago was a vital step toward fulfilling this obligation, and the Japanese Constitution, which embodies this axiom forever as the sovereign will[42] of a nation, should be a guiding light for the world in the 21st century.

Unfortunately, the Review Conference of the Nuclear Non-Proliferation Treaty this past May left no doubt that the U.S., Russia, U.K., France, China, India, Pakistan, North Korea and a few other nations wishing to become nuclear-weapon states are ignoring the majority voices of the people and governments of the world, thereby jeopardizing[43] human survival.

Based on the dogma "Might is right," these countries have formed their own "nuclear club," the admission requirement being possession of nuclear weapons. Through the media, they have long repeated the incantation[44], "Nuclear weapons protect you." With no means of rebuttal[45], many people worldwide have succumbed to[46] the feeling that "There is nothing we can do." Within the United Nations, nuclear club members use their veto power to override the global majority and pursue their selfish objectives.

---

39) Thou shalt not kill. 汝殺すことなかれ　40) [名]公理　41) [名]命題、必然的帰結　42) sovereign will 主権意思　43) jeopardize[他動]危うくする
44) [名]まじない　45) [名]反論　46) succumb to~ ～に屈服する

To break out of this situation, Mayors for Peace, with more than 1,080 member cities, is currently holding its sixth General Conference in Hiroshima, where we are revising the Emergency Campaign to Ban Nuclear Weapons launched two years ago. The primary objective is to produce an action plan that will further expand the circle of cooperation formed by the U.S. Conference of Mayors, the European Parliament, International Physicians for the Prevention of Nuclear War and other international NGOs, organizations and individuals worldwide, and will encourage all world citizens to awaken to their own responsibilities with a sense of urgency, "as if the entire world rests on their shoulders alone," and work with new commitment to abolish nuclear weapons.

To these ends and to ensure that the will of the majority is reflected at the UN, we propose that the First Committee of the UN General Assembly, which will meet in October, establish a special committee to deliberate and plan for the achievement and maintenance of a nuclear-weapon-free world. Such a committee is needed because the Conference on Disarmament in Geneva and the NPT Review Conference in New York have failed due to a "consensus rule" that gives a veto to every country.

We expect that the General Assembly will then act on the recommendations from this special committee, adopting by the year 2010 specific steps leading toward the elimination of nuclear weapons by 2020.

Meanwhile, we hereby declare the 369 days from today until August 9, 2006, a "Year of Inheritance, Awakening and Commitment[47]." During this Year, the Mayors for Peace, working with nations, NGOs and the vast majority of the world's people, will launch a great diversity of campaigns for nuclear weapons abolition in numerous cities throughout the world.

We expect the Japanese government to respect the voice of the world's cities and work energetically in the First Committee and the General Assembly to ensure that the abolition of nuclear weapons is achieved by the will of the majority. Furthermore, we request that the Japanese government provide the warm, humanitarian support appropriate to the needs of all the aging *hibakusha*, including those living abroad and those exposed in areas affected by the black rain.

On this, the sixtieth anniversary of the atomic bombing, we seek to comfort the souls of all its victims by declaring that we humbly reaffirm our responsibility never to "repeat the evil."

"Please rest peacefully; for we will not repeat the evil."

*   *   *

Peace Declaration (2004)

【Comments by the City of Hiroshima】
〈Declaring the one-year period ending on August 9,

---

47) Year of Inheritance, Awakening and Commitment 継承と目覚め、決意の年

2005 as a "Year of Remembrance and Action for a Nuclear-Free World"; resolving to abolish nuclear weapons by the year 2020; expressing expectation that as an expression of their love for humanity American citizens will discharge their duty as the lone superpower to eliminate nuclear weapons; expressing intent to promote the Hiroshima-Nagasaki Peace Study Course, implement projects to read eyewitness accounts of the atomic bombings, and deliver to the world the message of the atomic bomb survivors; demanding that the Japanese government defend the Peace Constitution and work diligently to rectify the trend toward open acceptance of war and nuclear weapons; appealing for support of the Emergency Campaign to Ban Nuclear Weapons, looking towards the NPT Review Conference⟩

"Nothing will grow for 75 years." Fifty-nine years have passed since the August sixth when Hiroshima was so thoroughly obliterated that many succumbed to such doom. Dozens of corpses still bearing the agony of that day, souls torn abruptly from their loved ones and their hopes for the future, have recently re-surfaced on Ninoshima Island, warning us to beware the utter inhumanity of the atomic bombing and the gruesome horror of war.

Unfortunately, the human race still lacks both a lexicon[48] capable of fully expressing that disaster and sufficient imagination to fill the gap. Thus, most of us float idly in the current of the day, clouding with self-

---

48) [名]語彙 (ごい)

indulgence[49] the lens of reason through which we should be studying the future, blithely[50] turning our backs on the courageous few.

As a result, the egocentric[51] worldview of the U.S. government is reaching extremes. Ignoring the United Nations and its foundation of international law, the U.S. has resumed research to make nuclear weapons smaller and more "usable." Elsewhere, the chains of violence and retaliation[52] know no end: reliance on violence-amplifying[53] terror and North Korea, among others, buying into the worthless policy of "nuclear insurance" are salient symbols of our times.

We must perceive and tackle this human crisis within the context of human history. In the year leading up to the 60th anniversary, which begins a new cycle of rhythms in the interwoven[54] fabric that binds humankind and nature, we must return to our point of departure, the unprecedented A-bomb experience. In the coming year, we must sow the seeds of new hope and cultivate a strong future-oriented movement.

To that end, the city of Hiroshima, along with the Mayors for Peace and our 611 member cities in 109 countries and regions, hereby declares the period beginning today and lasting until August 9, 2005, to be a Year of Remembrance and Action for a Nuclear-Free World. Our goal is to bring forth a beautiful "flower" for the 75th anniversary of the atomic bombings, namely, the total elimination of all nuclear weapons from the face of the Earth by the year 2020. Only then

---

49)［名］自分に甘いこと、自堕落　50)［副］軽率にも　51)［形］自己中心的な
52)［名］報復　53) violence-amplifying　暴力を拡大・増幅する　54)［形］織り合わされた

will we have truly resurrected[55] hope for life on this "nothing will grow" planet.

The seeds we sow today will sprout in May 2005. At the Review Conference for the Treaty on the Non-Proliferation of Nuclear Weapons (NPT) to be held in New York, the Emergency Campaign to Ban Nuclear Weapons will bring together cities, citizens, and NGOs from around the world to work with like-minded nations toward adoption of an action program that incorporates, as an interim goal, the signing in 2010 of a Nuclear Weapons Convention to serve as the framework for eliminating nuclear weapons by 2020.

Around the world, this Emergency Campaign is generating waves of support. This past February, the European Parliament passed by overwhelming majority a resolution specifically supporting the Mayors for Peace campaign. At its general assembly in June, the U.S. Conference of Mayors, representing 1183 U.S. cities, passed by acclamation[56] an even stronger resolution.

We anticipate that Americans, a people of conscience, will follow the lead of their mayors and form the mainstream of support for the Emergency Campaign as an expression of their love for humanity and desire to discharge their duty as the lone superpower to eliminate nuclear weapons.

We are striving to communicate the message of the *hibakusha* around the world and promote the Hiroshima-Nagasaki Peace Study Course to ensure,

---

55) resurrect［他動］復活させる　56) by acclamation 発声投票で

especially, that future generations will understand the inhumanity of nuclear weapons and the cruelty of war. In addition, during the coming year, we will implement a project that will mobilize adults to read eyewitness accounts of the atomic bombings to children everywhere.

The Japanese government, as our representative, should defend the Peace Constitution, of which all Japanese should be proud, and work diligently to rectify[57] the trend toward open acceptance of war and nuclear weapons increasingly prevalent at home and abroad. We demand that our government act on its obligation as the only A-bombed nation and become the world leader for nuclear weapons abolition, generating an anti-nuclear tsunami by fully and enthusiastically supporting the Emergency Campaign led by the Mayors for Peace. We further demand more generous relief measures to meet the needs of our aging *hibakusha*, including those living overseas and those exposed in black rain areas.

Rekindling the memory of Hiroshima and Nagasaki, we pledge to do everything in our power during the coming year to ensure that the 60th anniversary of the atomic bombings will see a budding of hope for the total abolition of nuclear weapons. We humbly offer this pledge for the peaceful repose of all atomic bomb victims.

* * *

57) rectify［他動］正す、修正する

Peace Declaration (2003)

【Comments by the City of Hiroshima】

〈Expressing concern over of the global trend toward the rule of power versus the rule of law, strongly criticizing the U.S. for forcing its will on the world; calling on the members of the Mayors for Peace to join in an emergency action to achieve the abolition of nuclear weapons through the NPT Review Conference: calling on influential leaders of the world to pray, speak, and act daily to bring about the abolition of nuclear weapons; demanding that the Japanese government make three new non-nuclear principles - "allow no production, al-low no possession, and allow no use of nuclear weapons" - national precepts; urging the Japanese government for the first time to provide support to all hibakusha, including those exposed in "black rain areas"〉

This year again, summer's heat reminds us of the blazing hell fire that swept over this very spot fifty-eight years ago. The world without nuclear weapons and beyond war that our *hibakusha* have sought for so long appears to be slipping deeper into a thick cover of dark clouds that they fear at any minute could become mushroom clouds spilling black rain.

The nuclear Non-Proliferation Treaty, the central international agreement guiding the elimination of nuclear weapons, is on the verge of [58] collapse. The

---

58) on the verge of ~ ～の瀬戸際にあって

chief cause is U.S. nuclear policy that, by openly declaring the possibility of a preemptive nuclear first strike[59] and calling for resumed research into mini-nukes and other so-called "useable nuclear weapons," appears to worship nuclear weapons as God.

However, nuclear weapons are not the only problem. Acting as if the United Nations Charter and the Japanese Constitution don't even exist, the world has suddenly veered sharply away from post-war toward pre-war mentality. As the U.S.-U.K.- led war on Iraq made clear, the assertion[60] that war is peace is being trumpeted as truth. Conducted with disregard for the multitudes around the world demanding a peaceful solution through continued UN inspections, this war slaughtered innocent women, children, and the elderly. It destroyed the environment, most notably through radioactive contamination[61] that will be with us for billions of years. And the weapons of mass destruction that served as the excuse for the war have yet to be found.

However, as President Lincoln once said, "You can't fool all the people all the time." Now is the time for us to focus once again on the truth that "Darkness can never be dispelled[62] by darkness, only by light." The rule of power is darkness. The rule of law is light. In the darkness of retaliation, the proper path for human civilization is illumined by the spirit of reconciliation born of the *hibakusha's* determination that "no one else should ever suffer as we did."

---

59) preemptive nuclear first strike 核兵器先制使用　60) [名]主張
61) radioactive contamination 放射能汚染　62) dispel[他動]追い散らす

Lifting up that light, the aging *hibakusha* are calling for U.S. President George Bush to visit Hiroshima. We all support that call and hereby demand that President Bush, Chairman Kim Jong Il of North Korea, and the leaders of all nuclear-weapon states come to Hiroshima and confront the reality of nuclear war. We must somehow convey to them that nuclear weapons are utterly evil, inhumane and illegal under international law.In the meanwhile, we expect that the facts about Hiroshima and Nagasaki will be shared throughout the world, and that the Hiroshima-Nagasaki Peace Study Course will be established in ever more colleges and universities.

To strengthen the NPT regime, the city of Hiroshima is calling on all members of the World Conference of Mayors for Peace to take emergency action to promote the abolition of nuclear weapons. Our goal is to gather a strong delegation of mayors representing cities throughout the world to participate in the NPT Review Conference that will take place in New York in 2005, the 60th year after the atomic bombing. In New York, we will lobby national delegates[63] for the start of negotiations at the United Nations on a universal Nuclear Weapons Convention providing for the complete elimination of nuclear weapons.

At the same time, Hiroshima calls on politicians, religious professionals, academics, writers, journalists, teachers, artists, athletes and other leaders with influence. We must establish a climate that immediately

---

63) [名]代表

confronts even casual comments that appear to approve of nuclear weapons or war. To prevent war and to abolish the absolute evil of nuclear weapons, we must pray, speak, and act to that effect in our daily lives.

The Japanese government, which publicly asserts its status as "the only A-bombed nation," must fulfill the responsibilities that accompany that status, both at home and abroad. Specifically, it must adopt as national precepts[64] the three new non-nuclear principles - allow no production, allow no possession, and allow no use of nuclear weapons anywhere in the world - and work conscientiously toward an Asian nuclear-free zone. It must also provide full support to all *hibakusha* everywhere, including those exposed in "black rain areas" and those who live overseas.

On this 58th August 6, we offer our heartfelt condolences to the souls of all atomic bomb victims, and we renew our pledge to do everything in our power to abolish nuclear weapons and eliminate war altogether by the time we turn this world over to our children.

*   *   *

Peace Declaration (2002)

【Comments by the City of Hiroshima】
〈Expressing grave concern that the world is locked in cycles of revenge and the logic of power; announcing plans to make Hiroshima a spiritual home for all people;

---

64) national precepts 国是

vowing to honor the collective human memory of Hiroshima and to make the 21st century a century of peace and humanity; urging the U.S. government and its people to renounce the logic of power; warning the Japanese government against making Japan a "normal country" capable of making war⟩

Another hot, agonizing summer has arrived for our *hibakusha* who, fifty-seven years ago, experienced "the end of the world," and, consequently, have worked tirelessly to bring peace to this world because "we cannot allow anyone else to go through that experience."

One reason for their agony, of course, is the annual reliving of that terrible tragedy.

In some ways more painful is the fact that their experience appears to be fading from the collective memory of humankind. Having never experienced an atomic bombing, the vast majority around the world can only vaguely imagine such horror, and these days, John Hersey's *Hiroshima* and Jonathan Schell's *The Fate of the Earth* are all but forgotten. As predicted by the saying, "Those who cannot remember the past are condemned to repeat it," the probability that nuclear weapons will be used and the danger of nuclear war are increasing.

Since the terrorist attack against the American people on September 11 last year, the danger has become more striking. The path of reconciliation--severing chains of hatred, violence and retaliation--so long advocated by the survivors has been abandoned. Today, the prevailing philosophy seems to be "I'll show you" and "I'm stronger than you are." In Afghanistan and the Middle East, in India and Pakistan, and wherever violent conflict erupts, the victims of this philosophy are overwhelmingly women, children, the elderly, and those least able to defend themselves.

President Kennedy said, "World peace...does not require that each man love his neighbor--it requires only that they live together with mutual tolerance[65]...." Within this framework of tolerance, we must all begin cooperating in any small way possible to build a common, brighter future for the human family. This is the meaning of reconciliation.

The spirit of reconciliation is not concerned with judging the past. Rather, it open-mindedly accepts human error and works toward preventing such errors in the future. To that end, conscientious exploration and understanding of the past is vital, which is precisely why we are working to establish the Hiroshima-Nagasaki Peace Study Course in colleges and universities around the world.

In the "spiritual home for all people" that Hiroshima is building grows an abundant Forest of Memory, and the River of Reconciliation and Humanity flowing from that forest is plied by Reason, Conscience and Compassion, ships that ultimately sail to the Sea of Hope and the Future.

I strongly urge President Bush to visit Hiroshima and

---

65) mutual tolerance 互いに寛容であること

Nagasaki to walk through that forest and ride that river. I beg him to encounter this human legacy[66] and confirm with his own eyes what nuclear weapons hold in store for us all.

The United States government has no right to force Pax Americana on the rest of us, or to unilaterally[67] determine the fate of the world. On the contrary, we, the people of the world, have the right to demand "no annihilation without representation[68]."

Article 99 of the Japanese Constitution stipulates that "The Emperor or the Regent as well as Ministers of State, members of the Diet, judges, and all other public officials have the obligation to respect and uphold this Constitution." The proper role of the Japanese government, under this provision, is to avoid making Japan a "normal country" capable of making war "like all the other nations." The government is bound to reject nuclear weapons absolutely and to renounce war[69]. Furthermore, the national government has a responsibility to convey the memories, voices, and prayers of Hiroshima and Nagasaki throughout the world, especially to the United States, and, for the sake of tomorrow's children, to prevent war.

The first step is to listen humbly to the *hibakusha* of the world. Assistance to all *hibakusha*, in particular to those dwelling overseas, must be enhanced to allow them to continue, in full security, to communicate their message of peace.

Today, in recalling the events of 57 years ago, we, the

---

66)［名］遺産　67)［副］一方的に　68) have the right to demand no annihilation without representation 人類を絶滅する権限を与えてはいないと主張する権利を持つ　69) renounce war 戦争を放棄する　※ renunciation of

people of Hiroshima, honor this collective human memory, vow to do our utmost to create a "century of peace and humanity," and offer our sincere prayers for the peaceful repose of all the atomic bomb victims.

*　　*　　*

Peace Declaration (2001)

【Comments by the City of Hiroshima】
〈First Peace Declaration of the 21st century; appealing for humankind to muster the courage to accept reconciliation and humanity as the way to create a century of peace and humanity, announcing intent to make Hiroshima soar to new heights as a city of humanity and a spiritual home for all people〉

On the first August sixth of the new century, we, the citizens of Hiroshima, living witnesses to "the century of war," hereby declare that we will do everything in our power to make the twenty-first century one of peace and humanity, free from nuclear weapons.

We believe that humanity means our willingness to listen to the voices of all sentient beings. Humanity also means nurturing children with loving care. It means valuing reconciliation in creating the human family's common future. It means rejecting violence and reaching peaceful agreements through the power of reason and conscience. Only humanity can assure the

war 戦争放棄

abolition of nuclear weapons; only humanity can ensure that nuclear weapons, once eliminated, are never re-invented.

In the twenty-first century, Hiroshima intends to soar to new heights as a city of humanity. We intend to create a spiritual home for all people, a home with compassion, a source of creativity and energy for our planet's children and youth, a city offering a personal place of rest and comfort for all, young or old, male and female.

However, the calendar end to "the century of war" has not automatically ushered[70] in a century of peace and humanity. Our world is still darkened not only by the direct violence of local conflicts and civil wars, but also by innumerable other forms of violence including environmental destruction, violence-promoting publications, images, and games. Now, through advanced science and technology, some are trying to extend battlefields into space.

We need our world leaders first to look at this reality humbly and unflinchingly[71]. They must also possess a strong will to eliminate nuclear weapons, sincerity in abiding by their agreements, which are crystallizations of human wisdom, and finally, the courage required to make reconciliation and humanity top priorities.

Many *hibakusha* and their kindred spirits, feeling called upon to shoulder the fate of the entire human race, have sought the abolition of nuclear weapons and world peace with a will strong enough to cut through solid rock. For *hibakusha*, the living hell suffered fifty-

---

70) usher [他動]案内する、先導する ※ usher in (時や時代の) 到来を告げる
71) [副]果敢に

six years ago remains vivid and present even today. Thus, communicating in living form to coming generations the *hibakusha's* memories, their sense of responsibility, and their unrelenting[72] will is the most dependable first step toward survival through the twenty-first century and on to the twenty-second century, connected by a bridge of hope.

To that end, the City of Hiroshima is investing in the revitalization[73] of peace education, in the broadest sense of that term. We are striving, in particular, to establish Hiroshima-Nagasaki peace study courses in major universities around the world. The basic framework for such courses will be constructed from the accomplishments of the Hiroshima Peace Institute and similar institutions where academic endeavour based on unalterable[74] fact have brought humankind closer to truth.

This week, the citizens of Hiroshima and Nagasaki are hosting the World Conference of Mayors for Peace through Inter-city Solidarity[75]. The conference has been organized for the expressed purpose of abolishing nuclear weapons and realizing world peace through truth-guided solidarity among cities, the entities that will carry most prominently the torch of humanity in the twenty-first century. It is no mere fantasy to believe that in the future, member cities of this conference will lead other municipalities in expanding the circle of nuclear-free authorities until ultimately the entire Earth becomes one solid nuclear free zone.

---

72)［形］たゆまない　73)［名］再活性化　74)［形］不変の　75) World Conference of Mayors for Peace through Inter-city Solidarity 世界平和連帯都市市長会議

Hiroshima calls on the national government of Japan to play an active role as a mediator in Asia in creating nuclear-free zones and implementing confidence-building measures. We further expect that, as a matter of national policy, Japan will initiate an effort to conclude a global treaty that prohibits nuclear weapons forever. We demand that our government properly value the contributions made by *hibakusha*, wherever they may live, which should culminate in[76] improved relief measures that respect their rights. Finally, we demand that our national government forge the will to abolish nuclear weapons and, in accordance with the preamble[77] of our constitution, work with Hiroshima in the effort to create a century of peace and humanity.

On this first August sixth of the twenty-first century, it is by vowing to spread the peace of this moment through the entire twenty-first century and throughout the world that we pay our sincerest respects to the souls of all the atomic bomb victims.

*   *   *

Peace Declaration (2000)

【Comments by the City of Hiroshima】
〈Looking back on the 20th century, a century in which scientific technology magnified the danger of war; appealing to the world to break chains of hatred and violence and clear a path to reconciliation; vowing that

---

76) culminate in~ 〜で終わる、最終的に〜になる   77) [名] 前文

> Hiroshima will make a new start as a city spreading the spirit of reconciliation through the world and exemplifying reconciliation between humankind and science and technology⟩

Today we are witnessing the last August sixth of the twentieth century.

It has been precisely fifty-five years since one single atomic bomb created a hell on earth. Together with the *hibakusha* who rose from the depths of despair, we have shed tears of wrenching[78] grief, comforted and encouraged each other, shared indignation and prayers, then studied and healed. Above all, we have appealed to the world through our actions. Our efforts have produced remarkable results in many respects: for example, we passed the Hiroshima Peace Memorial City Construction Law, constructed the Cenotaph for the A-bomb Victims, enacted the Atomic Bomb Survivors' Support Law, created a nuclear-free zone covering most of the Southern hemisphere, won a ruling by the International Court of Justice on the illegality of the use of nuclear weapons, concluded the Comprehensive Nuclear Test Ban Treaty, registered the Atomic Bomb Dome as a World Heritage site[79], and persuaded the nuclear-weapon states to agree to "An unequivocal undertaking...to accomplish the total elimination of their nuclear arsenals...." Of course, our most striking victory, for all humankind, is that nuclear weapons have not been used in war since Nagasaki.

---

78) [形]苦痛を伴う　79) World Heritage site 世界遺産

Unfortunately, our most fervent hope, to see nuclear weapons abolished by the end of this century, has not been realized.

We are determined, nevertheless, to overcome all obstacles and attain our goal in the twenty-first century. For this purpose also, it is imperative that[80] we reinterpret the *hibakusha* experience in a broader context, find ever more effective ways to express its significance, and carry on the legacy as a universal human heritage. Our effort to preserve and utilize the Atomic Bomb Dome, now officially designated a World Heritage site, the former Bank of Japan Hiroshima Branch, which withstood the bomb's blast, and the many paper cranes sent by children from all over the world is important in this regard. It is also crucial that we mobilize the World Conference of Mayors for Peace through Inter-city Solidarity to translate the ruling that "nuclear weapons are illegal" into their abolition. Furthermore, we will continue to call on individuals everywhere to recognize whatever responsibility their own countries or ethnic groups may bear for war, to do everything in their power to break the chain of hatred and violence, to set out bravely on the road to reconciliation, and to ensure that the world abolishes all nuclear weapons without delay.

Looking back to ancient times - long before there were computers, pencils, or even written language - the twentieth century is distinguished from previous centuries by the fact that our science and technology

---

80) it is imperative that~　～が絶対に必要だ、急務である

have created concrete dangers that threaten the very existence of humankind. Nuclear weapons are one such danger. Global environmental degradation[81] is another. They are both problems that we have brought upon ourselves, and both are problems that we must act responsibly to resolve.

Having called on the world to abolish nuclear weapons, Hiroshima wishes to make a new start as a model city demonstrating the use of science and technology for human purposes. We will create a future in which Hiroshima itself is the embodiment[82] of those "human purposes." We will create a twenty-first century in which Hiroshima's very existence formulates the substance of peace. Such a future would exemplify a genuine reconciliation between humankind and the science and technology that have endangered our continued survival.

The north-south summit meeting on the Korean Peninsula was an outstanding example of human reconciliation. Patterned after the exchange of cherry trees and dogwood trees symbolic of Japan-U.S. friendship early in this century, Hiroshima would like, with the cooperation of both Japanese and American citizens, to create its own dogwood promenade symbolic of all such reconciliations. On the international stage, Hiroshima aspires to serve as a mediator actively creating reconciliation by helping to resolve conflict and animosity.

Again we call upon the government of Japan to

---

81) environmental degradation 環境悪化　82) [名]具現化

recognize the crucial role that the *hibakusha* have played and to further enhance its support policies for them. In addition, we strongly call upon the government to forge the collective will to advocate the abolition of nuclear weapons and make common cause with Hiroshima for global reconciliation in accordance with the preamble to our Constitution.

Gathered here in Hiroshima on the last August sixth of the twentieth century, as our thoughts turn to humanity's past and future, we declare our resolve that, if we had only one pencil we would continue to write first of the sanctity[83] of human life and then of the need to abolish nuclear weapons. Last but certainly not least, we pay our profound respects to the souls of all who perished in the tragedy of Hiroshima.

＊　　＊　　＊

Peace Declaration (1999)

【Comments by the City of Hiroshima】
〈Looking back on Hiroshima's history, expressing gratitude to the *hibakusha* for their contribution; emphasizing the paramount importance of world leaders forging the will to abolish nuclear weapons〉

A century of war, the twentieth century spawned[84] the devil's own weapons - nuclear weapons - and humankind has yet to free itself of their threat.

83) [名]尊厳、神聖さ、高潔さ　84) spawn[他動]生む、大量に発生させる

Nonetheless, inspired by the memory of the hundreds of thousands who died so tragically in Hiroshima and Nagasaki and all of war's victims, we have fought for the fifty-four years since those bombings for the total abolition of nuclear weapons.

It is the many courageous *hibakusha* and the people who have identified with their spirit who have led this struggle. Looking at the important contributions these *hibakusha* have made, we cannot but express our deepest gratitude to them.

There are three major contributions:

The first is that they were able to transcend the infernal pain and despair that the bombings sowed and to opt for[85] life. I want young people to remember that today's elderly *hibakusha* were as young as they are when their families, their schools, and their communities were destroyed in a flash. They hovered between life and death in a corpse-strewn[86] sea of rubble and ruin-circumstances[87] under which none would have blamed them had they chosen death. Yet they chose life. We should never forget the will and courage that made it possible for the *hibakusha* to continue to be human.

Their second accomplishment is that they effectively prevented a third use of nuclear weapons. Whenever conflict and war break out, there are those who advocate nuclear weapon's use. This was true even in Kosovo. Yet the *hibakusha's* will that the evil not be repeated has prevented the unleashing of this lunacy[88]. Their

---

85) opt for~　～を選ぶ　86) corpse-strewn　死屍累々の、死体が散乱した
87) ruin-circumstances 破滅的状況　88) [名]愚行、狂気の沙汰

determination to tell their story to the world, to argue eloquently[89] that to use nuclear weapons is to doom the human race, and to show the use of nuclear weapons to be the ultimate evil has brought about this result. We owe our future and our children's future to them.

Their third achievement lies in their representing the new worldview as engraved on[90] the Cenotaph[91] for the A-bomb Victims and articulated in the Japanese Constitution. They have rejected the path of revenge and animosity that leads to extinction for all humankind. Instead, they have taken upon themselves not only the evil that Japan as a nation perpetrated but also the evil of war itself. They have also chosen to put their "trust in the justice and faith" of all humankind in order to create a future full of hope. As peace-loving people from all over the world solemnly[92] proclaimed at the Hague Appeal for Peace Conference this May, this is the path that humankind should take in the new century. We ardently[93] applaud all of the countries and people who have written this philosophy into their Constitutions and their laws.

Above all else, we must possess a strong will to abolish nuclear weapons following the examples set by the *hibakusha*. If all the world shares this commitment - indeed, even if only the leaders of the nuclear weapons states will it so - nuclear weapons can be eliminated tomorrow.

Such will is born of truth - the truth that nuclear weapons are the absolute evil and cause humankind's

---

89) ［副］とうとうと、雄弁に　90) A is engraved on B AがBに刻み込まれている
91) the Cenotaph 世界大戦戦没者記念碑、ここでは原爆死没者慰霊碑のこと
92) ［副］おごそかに　93) ［副］熱烈に

extinction.

Where there is such will, there is a way. Where there is such determination, any path we take leads to our goal of eliminating nuclear weapons. However, if we lack the will to take the first step, we can never reach our goal no matter how easy the way. I especially hope our young people share this will.

Thus, we again call upon the government of Japan to understand fully the crucial role the *hibakusha* have played and to enhance their support policies. We also call upon the government to place the highest priority on forging the will to abolish nuclear weapons. It is imperative that the government of Japan follow the philosophy outlined in the preamble of the Constitution to persuade other countries of this course and cement a global commitment to the abolition of nuclear weapons. I declare the abolition of nuclear weapons to be our most important responsibility for the future of the earth, and pay my utmost respect to the souls of the many who perished in the atomic bombings. May they rest in peace.

CHAPTER 3

TAKASHI HIRAOKA's[1] PEACE DECLARATION

(1998–1991)

Peace Declaration (1998)

【Comments by the City of Hiroshima】
〈Protest against the nuclear tests conducted by India and Pakistan; calling for the conclusion of a "treaty for the non-use of nuclear weapons"; mention about the establishment of the Hiroshima Peace Institute〉

Fifty-three years after the tragedy of Hiroshima, states remain deeply distrustful of each other and the world is on the brink of a new crisis.

With the nuclear tests by first India and then Pakistan, tension has been raised to new extremes in Southwest Asia and the nuclear non-proliferation regime has been shaken to its core. Having consistently argued nuclear weapons' inherent inhumanity and called upon the world for their abolition, Hiroshima is outraged at the two states' nuclear tests and fearful that they might provoke a chain reaction of nuclearization[2].

Contributing to this situation is the fact that the five declared nuclear states have clung to nuclear deterrence

1) 平岡敬(市長任期1991年2月～1999年2月)　2) [名] 核軍備競争、核武装化

theory and made only glacial progress on the nuclear disarmament negotiations mandated under the Nuclear Non-proliferation Treaty. The leaders of the nuclear states need to focus not on their own narrow national interests but on the future of humanity and need to fulfill their responsibilities to the international community as soon as possible.

The world cries out for new wisdom and new patterns of behavior. In keeping with the spirit of the advisory opinion issued by the International Court of Justice, all countries should immediately initiate negotiations on a treaty for the nonuse of nuclear weapons as one step on the road to these weapons' total abolishment.

We implore the government of Japan, the first country to suffer atomic bombing, to take the lead in effectively pressing the nuclear states for the abolition of nuclear weapons. At the same time, I believe it is imperative that all Japanese give serious thought to security policies that are not nuclear-dependent.

Many people throughout the world today still suffer from the aftermath of nuclear tests and other exposure. Their plight[3], together with Hiroshima's experience, makes the issues we face in this nuclear age explicit. Hiroshima is working to establish and strengthen interpersonal and intercity ties transcending national borders, and we hope that this network can impact international politics to create a nuclear-free world.

Hiroshima has long engaged in grass-roots cultural exchanges, held atomic bomb awareness exhibitions in

---

3) ［名］(悪い) 状態、窮状

Japan and overseas, promoted the formation of the World Conference of Mayors for Peace through Inter-city Solidarity, and otherwise sought to contribute to marshaling[4] international public opinion in the cause of peace. This spring, we established the Hiroshima Peace Institute and began work on creating a better future for all the world. All of this has been consistent with Hiroshima's desire to be the world's "peace capital."

"Everyone has the right to life, liberty and security of person." So states the Universal Declaration of Human Rights. Yet the current nuclear arsenals with their devastating consequences for all humanity compel us, 50 years after the Declaration's adoption, to reconsider our culture's infatuation with science and technology and to renew our commitment to working to create an international community in which the right to life is our highest priority.

On this 53rd Peace Memorial Day, I would like to offer our utmost respects to the souls of those who died from the atomic bombing and to call for compassionate assistance for all *hibakusha* responsive to their actual situations whether in Japan and overseas.

In closing, I proclaim anew that we are determined to act resolutely in the spirit of renouncing nuclear weapons so that all nations can escape the folly[5] of relying on nuclear force for their security as soon as possible.

---

4) marshal［他動］先導する、集結させる　5) ［名］愚かさ

*   *   *

Peace Declaration (1997)

【Comments by the City of Hiroshima】
〈Unease concerning the future of the scientific and technological civilization; protest against US subcritical nuclear testing; requesting that the Japanese government work to construct a security structure that does not rely on a "nuclear umbrella"〉

It was 52 years ago today that a single atomic bomb exploded over Hiroshima. The skies flashed brighter than a thousand suns and a huge mushroom cloud rose above the city. Untold numbers perished in the sea of flames that followed, and the survivors still suffer from radiation's debilitating[6] aftereffects.

This event engendered[7] profound distrust of the scientific civilization that has made such dramatic progress over the last hundred years. Science and technology have spawned many conveniences and made our lives more comfortable, yet they have also been employed to create the weapons of mass destruction used over Hiroshima and Nagasaki. Not only do nuclear weapons imperil humanity's future, the civilization that created them gravely impacts the whole of the global ecosystem.

We in Hiroshima are outraged that nuclear weapons have yet to be abolished and banished from the face of

6) debilitate［他動］衰弱させる　7) engender［他動］発生させる

the earth, and we are very uneasy about the future of civilization.

In signing the Comprehensive Test Ban Treaty, the international community agreed to put a halt to all nuclear explosions, but much remains to be done before the CTBT can go into force[8]. This was the situation when the United States conducted a subcritical test which it contends is not banned by the CTBT language. On the one hand, the U.S. promises to reduce its stockpiles of nuclear weapons, and on the other hand it obstinately[9] maintains its nuclear testing program. This attitude is utterly devoid of the wisdom needed if all peoples are to co-exist. We implore the global community to recognize that nuclear weapons stand at the very apex of [10] all of the violence that war represents.

The Fourth World Conference of Mayors for Peace through Inter-city Solidarity currently meeting in Hiroshima seeks a nuclear-free world and is deliberating calling upon all governments and international institutions to conclude a pact banning the use of nuclear weapons and to expand nuclear-weapons-free zones. Hiroshima specifically calls upon the government of Japan to devise security arrangements that do not rely upon a nuclear umbrella.

Japan and other countries differ in language, religion, and customs, and there are also some differences of historical perspective, particularly with our neighbors. All the more do we hope that candid dialogue among all the peoples of the world will result in a shared vision

---

8) go into force 効力を発する、発効する 9) [副]がんこに、しつこく 10) at the very apex of~ ～の頂点にあって

of a brighter tomorrow.

With the world in tumultuous[11] transition, we intend to take every opportunity at home and abroad to convey not only the terrible violence, destruction, and death the atomic bomb wrought[12] but also the inspiring beauty of human life striving toward the future despite experiencing abject despair. The culture of peace generated in the process of Hiroshima's rebirth is a beacon of hope for all humanity, just as the Atomic Bomb Dome, now designated a World Heritage site, stands as a symbol of hope for all who reject nuclear weapons.

Along with paying our utmost respects to the souls of those who died, we pledge ourselves anew on this Peace Memorial Day to pressing for compassionate assistance policies grounded in reality for the aging *hibakusha* wherever they may live.

"Since wars begin in the minds of men, it is in the minds of men that the defenses of peace must be constructed." This thought from the UNESCO (United Nations Educational, Scientific and Cultural Organization) Constitution must be indelibly[13] etched in our hearts, and I hereby declare it Hiroshima's resolve.

*   *   *

---

11) ［形］激動の　12) workの過去形［他動］引き起こす、生じさせる　13) ［副］永久に

Peace Declaration (1996)

【Comments by the City of Hiroshima】
〈Declaration by the International Court of Justice on the illegality of the use of nuclear weapons; hopes for the Comprehensive Nuclear Test Ban Treaty; statement that the lives and the deaths following the bombing of Hiroshima must touch hearts and that this culture of peace must become part of humanity's shared legacy; necessity of archiving the extensive documentation on the bombing〉

No matter how many months and years may pass, the memory of Hiroshima lives on in our hearts.

Now more than half a century since that cataclysm[14], the world still faces the threat of nuclear weapons. Yet we refuse to abandon hope and will continue to argue that humanity cannot co-exist with nuclear weapons.

Even though the East-West conflict has ended, the nuclear powers continue to maintain their arsenals, and the dependence on military force that distrust and suspicion prompt does nothing to guarantee our security. Peace is shattered when disputes, poverty, discrimination, and other ills are exacerbated by military force. Nuclear weapons symbolize all the violence that obstructs peace.

Albeit only in general terms, the International Court of Justice has declared the use of nuclear weapons illegal. Gradually, inexorably, public opinion favoring

---

14) ［名］惨禍

the elimination of nuclear weapons is spreading worldwide. We hope that this rising tide will compel agreement on a new Comprehensive Nuclear Test Ban Treaty prohibiting all nuclear explosions, of which there have been more than 2,000, and leading to a total ban on nuclear tests. At the same time, however, given the uncertain prospects for the elimination of nuclear weapons, we are deeply concerned that the nuclear powers are consolidating[15] their arsenals.

As the next step, we thus intend to join in solidarity with the entire international community for a universal convention[16] prohibiting the use of nuclear weapons and to work here at home for legislation formalizing Japan's non-nuclear status.

Another urgent imperative in the quest for peace is that of continuing to explain the realities of history's first atomic bombing and to see that these are conveyed across national and generational differences. The experiences, both the lives and the deaths, following the bombing of Hiroshima must be refined so they touch every heart and this culture of peace becomes part of humanity's shared legacy.

It is also essential that the extensive documentation on the bombing be archived. I hope that younger generations, far-removed as they are from the wartime realities and the bombing's horrors, will be inspired by the insights and impressions that they draw from the *hibakusha* testimonies and other documentation.

At the same time. I want to find policies for supporting

---

15) consolidate[他動]固定する、強固にする   16) universal convention 国際
条約

the aging *hibakusha* in Japan and elsewhere commensurate with[17] their real needs.

Marking the 51st anniversary of the bombing, we here today both pay our sincere respects to the souls of those *hibakusha* who died and renew our vow to work untiringly[18] for the elimination of all nuclear weapons and for peace. Fully cognizant of Japanese history and in the spirit of the Constitution, I also pledge to work with the people of Hiroshima to make Hiroshima a creative, hopeful city of peace.

*   *   *

Peace Declaration (1995)

【Comments by the City of Hiroshima】
〈Assertion that the atomic bomb is clearly an inhumane weapon that violates international law; call to establish a new nuclear-free zone in the Asian-Pacific region; assertion that war must be reexamined from the perspectives of both perpetrator and victim to enable a common understanding of history〉

It is now half a century to the day since Hiroshima was devastated by the atomic bomb. Along with recalling that fateful day and praying for the souls of the many who died, and being acutely aware of the difficulties the aging *hibakusha* face, I cannot but repeat in the strongest possible terms that the development

---

17) commensurate with〜　〜に釣り合って、〜にふさわしく　18) [副]根気よく、たゆまずに

and possession of nuclear weapons constitutes a crime against humanity.

Throughout this half-century, we have told all the world of the human devastation that the atomic bombs wrought, particularly the unprecedented damage of radiation, in a consistent appeal that nuclear weapons be abolished. Yet distrust among nations is deep-rooted and there are vast stockpiles of nuclear weapons around the globe, creating a formidable barrier to the attainment of our ideal. It is profoundly saddening that some people see the possession of nuclear weapons as symbolic of a nation's strength.

Nuclear weapons are clearly inhumane weapons in obvious violation of international law. So long as such weapons exist, it is inevitable that the horror of Hiroshima and Nagasaki will be repeated - somewhere, sometime - in an unforgivable affront[19] to humanity itself.

If humanity is to maintain hope for the future, we must act now with courage and decisiveness to achieve a nuclear-free world. As a first step, we call for an immediate and comprehensive nuclear test ban and the establishment of a new nuclear-free zone in the Asia-Pacific. In keeping with the Constitution's pacifist ideals and proclaiming its three non-nuclear principles (of non-possession, non-manufacture, and non-introduction[20]), the government of Japan should take the lead in working for the abolition of nuclear weapons. Likewise, we also call upon the government to be more

---

19) ［名］侮辱　20) non-possession, non-manufacture, and non-introduction 持たず、作らず、持ち込ませず

supportive of all *hibakusha* - these witnesses to the nuclear era - in Japan and elsewhere.

The possession of nuclear weapons is no guarantee of national security. Rather, the proliferation of nuclear weapons, the transfer of nuclear weapons technology, and the leakage of nuclear materials are all threats to the survival of the human race. Like the suppression[21] of human rights, impoverishment and starvation, regional conflict, and the destruction of the global environment, these are all major threats to world peace.

This is an era in which we must think of global security. It is a time to foster human solidarity transcending national borders, to pool our wisdom, and to work together to establish world peace.

At this 50th anniversary of the end of World War II, it is important to look at the stark reality of war in terms of both aggrieved and aggriever[22] so as to develop a common understanding of history. The suffering of all the war's victims indelibly etched in our hearts, we want to apologize for the unbearable suffering that Japanese colonial domination and war inflicted on so many people.

Memory is where past and future meet. Respectfully learning the lessons of the past, we want to impress the misery of war and the atomic bombing on the generations of younger people who will be tomorrow's leaders. Similarly, we also need to emphasize the human aspects of education as the basis for peace. Only when life and human rights are accorded the highest priority

21)［名］抑圧　22) aggrieved and aggriever　被害 (者) と加害 (者)

can young people enjoy lives of boundless hope.

At this Peace Memorial Ceremony commemorating the 50th anniversary of the atomic bombing, I am resolved to spare no effort in achieving the abolition of nuclear Weapons and the attainment of world peace.

*　　*　　*

Peace Declaration (1994)

【Comments by the City of Hiroshima】
〈Significance of the A-bomb Dome becoming a World Heritage; opposition to the indefinite extension of the Nuclear Non-Proliferation Treaty〉

The sun was dazzling[23] bright that summer morning when a single atomic bomb instantly destroyed this town of Hiroshima and took its deadly toll[24]. And it pains me to be unable to stand before this monument to those dead and to report to them that we finally have a world free of nuclear weapons.

It is now nearly half a century since that fateful day, and the present is a time of major transition, for the world at large and also for Japan, as we move from an era of conflict to an era of concert. Yet the world still bristles with nuclear weapons. Hiroshima, along with Nagasaki, appeals to the leaders of all nuclear-armed countries to promptly announce the elimination of their nuclear weapons. The world's leaders must

---

23) dazzle[他動]目をくらませる　24) [名]犠牲者 ※take a toll 多くの人の命を奪う

understand that the development and possession of nuclear weapons is a crime against humanity. Thus we hope to have the Atomic Bomb Dome registered as part of the world's cultural heritage so that it can stand as a warning to all humankind.

Nuclear weapons - weapons of wide-spread and indiscriminate destruction and releasing massive doses of deadly radiation - are patently illegal under international law. This is something that the *hibakusha* know from personal experience. While the International Court of Justice is moving to review the legality of the use of nuclear weapons, we fervently hope the world will see the reality of Hiroshima and Nagasaki and will fully recognize the inhumanity of nuclear weapons.

As I stated at the Second United Nations Conference on Disarmament Issues in Hiroshima, we are opposed to the indefinite extension of a Nuclear Non-Proliferation Treaty that makes no clear provisions for the elimination of nuclear weapons and perpetuates the uneasy relationship between the nuclear-weapon states and the non-nuclear-weapon states. The Japanese Government should take specific steps to demonstrate its opposition to nuclear weapons in global forums, including seeking to extend the three non-nuclear principles (of non-possession, non-manufacture, and non-introduction) to the international community and promoting the establishment of a nuclear-free zone in Northeast Asia, so as to fulfill the responsibilities incumbent upon[25] it as a country that has suffered atomic bombing.

Noting how Hiroshima has overcome the tragedy of atomic bombing and is able to play host to the 12th Asian Games this October, one of the countries planning to take part in the Games characterized Hiroshima as a symbol of mankind's hopes for peace. These words give us new pride and confidence - although we must obviously never forget Japan's war against and colonial domination of the other nations of Asia.

Accidents at nuclear power plants, radioactive waste disposal, and the like pollute the entire world irrespective of political borders. It is thus all the more important that we have international transparency regarding the management of radioactive materials[26], particularly plutonium, and that nuclear power technology be subject to the controlling principles of democracy, independence, and transparency.

Having lived nearly 50 years with their affliction, the *hibakusha* are most anxious to have Japan enact the *Hibakusha* Relief Law for a better future. Now is the time for Japan to initiate far-reaching[27] relief policies based upon the spirit of national indemnification[28] for all *hibakusha*, regardless of who they are or where they live.

History is the tale of humankind's struggle to create a society in which people do not quake before the terror of war, do not suffer from poverty and malnutrition[29], and are not exposed to discrimination and prejudice. It

25) incumbent on~ 〜の義務である　26) radioactive materials 放射性物質
27)［形］遠大な　28) national indemnification 国家補償　29)［名］栄養失調

is imperative that we continue to speak to young people everywhere of the horrors of war and Hiroshima's atomic bombing and hence of our dreams for the future.

At this ceremony commemorating the 49th anniversary of the atomic bombing of Hiroshima, I would thus like both to pay my sincere respects to the spirits of the dead here and to declare anew my determination to focus the energies of the people of Hiroshima for the building of a world of peace.

*   *   *

Peace Declaration (1993)

【Comments by the City of Hiroshima】
〈Warning against the movement for indefinite extension of the Nuclear Non-Proliferation Treaty; request to the Japanese government to promptly settle post-war treatment issues〉

August 6th, the day the people of Hiroshima can never forget, has come again. In recalling the living hell that arose in our city forty-eight years ago, we strongly appeal to the conscience of the world in declaring that the development and possession of nuclear weapons is a sin against humanity.

Since the tragedy that befell[30] Hiroshima and Nagasaki, nuclear weapons have not been used nor

---

30) befall［他動］起こる、ふりかかる

have they accidentally exploded, yet there is no guarantee that such things will never happen in the future.

Recently, the United States, Russia, and France have extended the moratorium on nuclear testing. Although this is a step in the right direction, nuclear weapons are still piled up in great numbers on this planet and pose a grave threat to humankind.

Therefore, as we declared this April at the United Nations NGO Special Session Devoted to Disarmament, we hereby express our great fear of the move by the countries with nuclear weapons to extend indefinitely the Nuclear Non-Proliferation Treaty, which is due to expire in 1995. While admitting that the treaty so far has played an important role, its indefinite extension would not only destabilize relations between the countries with nuclear weapons and those without them, but this would also run counter to[31] our hopes for the abolition of nuclear weapons. Today, the lack of transparency surrounding nuclear power development on the Korean Peninsula and elsewhere is causing uneasiness in the world. The nuclear powers, while observing a comprehensive ban on nuclear testing and honoring the Nuclear Non-Proliferation Treaty, should set the goal of total abolition of all nuclear weapons and announce to the world a target date of no later than the year 2000.

We must allow no more environmental contamination caused by accidents at nuclear power plants or the

---

31) run counter to~ ～に背く

dumping [32]of nuclear waste. Although there has been remarkable technological progress in the peaceful utilization of nuclear power, it is of urgent necessity, from the standpoint of the principle of safety first, to set up an international control system for radioactive material, specifically plutonium, and to ensure transparency at the global level.

With the Asian Games scheduled to take place in Hiroshima in the fall of 1994, what other Asian peoples think of Japan is of direct concern to us. We honestly acknowledge and sincerely regret that our nation in the past, during its colonial rule and in wartime activities, inflicted on people throughout the Asia-Pacific region severe hardships, the scars of which remain deep in their hearts. And we are especially distressed when we contemplate the intense suffering since the war of the many victims of the atomic bombings now living on the Korean Peninsula. In order for us to establish everlasting ties of friendship with the peoples of the Asia-Pacific region, it is imperative that the Japanese Government settle quickly those issues from the post-war period that remain unresolved.

The 3rd World Conference of Mayors for Peace through Inter-city Solidarity is now convening in Hiroshima. In striving for a world free of nuclear weapons and war, the cities participating in the conference are working to marshal international public opinion and are discussing various actions that might be taken in this regard.

---

32) [名]投棄

With each passing year, the victims of the atomic bombings residing in Japan and abroad, who directly experienced its inhumanity, are growing older. Today, almost half a century after the atomic bombing, it is more urgent than ever that the Government of Japan, in the spirit of take measures to assist these individuals, both materially and spiritually.

At the same time, we must improve the way we educate future generations regarding the history of the atomic bombing and the war. It is a barrenness[33] of spirit that stands in the way of the creation of peace.

Here at the Peace Memorial Ceremony to commemorate the 48th anniversary of the atomic bombing of Hiroshima, we wish to express our profound condolences for the souls of the victims of the atomic bombing, to continue working toward the establishment of eternal peace, and to pledge ourselves to the promotion of an even deeper understanding of all that "Hiroshima" stands for.

* * *

Peace Declaration (1992)

【Comments by the City of Hiroshima】
〈Clear rejection of the argument of nuclear deterrence; report on the UN Conference on Disarmament Issues in Hiroshima〉

---

33) [名]不毛

It is now forty-seven years since that fateful day when Hiroshima was devastated by a single atomic explosion and countless of its citizens perished. Never can we forget the horrible sights that assailed[34] our eyes under Hiroshima's mushroom cloud.

Carrying that memory, we have been untiring in our appeal for the abolition of nuclear weapons and the establishment of lasting world peace so that the horror of Hiroshima never again be repeated.

Yet nuclear testing continues even today. Hiroshima cannot condone a policy of nuclear deterrence that makes national security hostage to nuclear weapons. Nor is the problem only nuclear weapons, as massive arsenals of biological, chemical, and other weapons of mass destruction have been built up over the years to cast a dark shadow over the future of humankind.

The world is now at a historic turning point with the dissolution[35] of the Soviet Union and other dramatic changes. Even though the basic structure of the Cold War between East and West has collapsed and the United States and Russia have reached agreement on deep cuts in their nuclear arsenals, we are still at a crossroads asking whether humankind will opt for conciliation and cooperation or will again revert to confrontation and conflict.

It is absolutely imperative that we halt the proliferation of nuclear weapons and the spread of nuclear technology. There is also an urgent need to establish a system of nuclear inspections and to deal safely with

---

34) assail［他動］攻撃する　35)［名］消滅

the radioactive materials left over as nuclear warheads are dismantled.

This June, Hiroshima had the honor of hosting the long-awaited United Nations Conference on Disarmament Issues in Hiroshima. Among the means that Hiroshima proposed at that Conference to promote the abolition of nuclear weapons were an immediate and comprehensive nuclear test ban, disclosure of the status of all nuclear arsenals, the holding of the Fourth Special Session of the United Nations General Assembly Devoted to Disarmament commemorating the fiftieth anniversary of the bombing of Hiroshima, and the establishment of a permanent forum in Hiroshima for discussing disarmament and confidence-building measures in the Asia-Pacific region. We hope that these proposals will be given serious study within and without the United Nations and that they will be implemented as soon as possible.

In addition to being threatened with nuclear annihilation, our survival is today also imperiled by the degradation of the global environment. Seeking to preserve the conditions for safe and comfortable living, we intend to develop a new self-awareness as human beings transcending race and nationality and to create a world of peace.

Thus it is that Hiroshima is further strengthening the inter-city bonds of solidarity for peace and building a wide range of friendly and cooperative relations. In addition, we want to further enhance relief efforts for *hibakusha* around the world.

Japan inflicted great hardship and suffering on the peoples of the Asia-Pacific region during its long period of war and colonization. Empathizing with this suffering, we must further strengthen our ties of community for the future. Rectitude[36] must be the foundation of trust.

On this forty-seventh anniversary of that tragic bombing, we earnestly pray for the repose of the many victims of the bombing and vow that "we shall not repeat the evil." At the same time, we very much hope that the government of Japan will enact the *Hibakusha* Relief Law under the principle of national indemnification for those people who died that day for peace and the aged *hibakusha* who continue to suffer the after-effects of radiation and will also endeavor to assist those *hibakusha* who are resident overseas as well.

The road to abolishing nuclear weapons and establishing a new order of peace is still long and arduous. Now more than ever must each and every one of us rid ourselves of prejudice and hatred and have the strength to sustain the cause of peace. We do hereby pledge ourselves anew to defending the ideal of non-belligerence[37] embodied in the Constitution of Japan and to continuing to inform young people everywhere of Hiroshima's central significance for peace.

*   *   *

36) ［名］公正、道義　37) ［名］不戦

Peace Declaration (1991)

【Comments by the City of Hiroshima】
⟨First use of the expression, "*hibakusha*"; first Peace Declaration of Mayor Takashi Hiraoka; apology to the people in the Asia-Pacific region; regret for the Persian Gulf War; first use of expression "*Hibakusha* Relief Law"⟩

August 6 is a profoundly sad day for the people of Hiroshima. Yet it is also a day of renewing our dedication to peace and a day that we hope will live forever in the world's memory.

Forty-six years ago today, Hiroshima was devastated and countless lives were lost as the result of a single atomic bomb. This was the first wartime use of nuclear weapons in human history. Knowing from bitter experience how very easily the use of nuclear weapons could lead to the extinction of the human race, Hiroshima has sought untiringly to transcend hardship and hatred and to call unwaveringly[38] for the abolition of all nuclear weapons and the attainment of lasting world peace.

Humanity has, just barely, escaped the hel1 of nuclear wars in the years since then, but the dangers of radioactive exposure have spread worldwide with the reckless nuclear testing and the accidents at atomic power plants. No more. We must generate no more *hibakusha*.

---

38) [副]断固たる決心で

Hiroshima has begun to extend medical assistance to the victims of Chernobyl and other nuclear disasters, but their numbers are vast indeed. Thus it is that, taking this leadership initiative, Hiroshima is calling for an international relief effort for these people.

Iraq's invasion of Kuwait last year was completely beyond the bounds of acceptability. Yet the ensuing Gulf War not only generated vast numbers of casualties[39] and refugees but also sparked environmental destruction threatening to destroy the global ecosystem. It is essential that we establish the means for peaceful conflict resolution.

Japan inflicted great suffering and despair on the peoples of Asia and the Pacific during its reign of colonial domination and war. There can be no excuse for these actions. This year marks the 50th anniversary of the start of the Pacific War. Remembering all too well the horror of this war starting with the attack on Pearl Harbor and ending with the atomic bombings of Hiroshima and Nagasaki, we are determined anew to work for world peace.

Peace, of course, is more than the mere absence of war. Achieving peace also means eliminating starvation, poverty, violence, threats to human rights, refugee problems, global environmental pollution, and the many other threats to peace, and it means creating a climate in which people can live rich and rewarding lives.

The world is today groping[40] its way toward a new

39) [名] 死傷者   40) grope [他動] 手探りでさがす

world order successor to the Cold War. Major progress has been made toward nuclear disarmament. The heavy portals barring the way to peace are slowly being opened, and they can only be opened fully with the weight of our collective wisdom and concerted efforts.

Hiroshima thus renews its appeal:

Let all nations everywhere put an immediate and complete end to nuclear testing arid strive for the earliest possible abolition of nuclear arms.

Let all peoples everywhere recognize the folly and futility[41] of war, reaffirm the treasure of peace, and work together for human happiness.

Hiroshima's appeal is a plaintive cry for the preservation of the human race, and we hope that the world's leaders will heed this plea.

It is imperative that we give most careful consideration to the different modalities[42] of international cooperation and that we contribute to true world peace. It is essential that we observe the principles of peace embedded in[43] our Constitution and promote education that inculcates[44] a feeling for the preciousness of peace. It is essential that the *Hibakusha* Relief Law be promptly instituted under the principle of national indemnification. At the same time, we earnestly hope that forthright efforts will be made to promote support for those *hibakusha* resident on the Korean Peninsula, in the United States, and elsewhere. We call upon the government of Japan to do more in all of these areas.

Today, in this Peace Memorial Ceremony to

---

41) [名]愚かさ　42) [名]手順　43) be embedded in~ 〜に組み込まれている
44) inculcate[他動]植え付ける、教え込む

commemorate the 46th anniversary of the atomic bombing of Hiroshima, I would like to express my heartfelt condolences to all of the victims of that bombing and to pledge myself to join the people of Hiroshima in working untiringly for peace.

CHAPTER 4

TAKESHI ARAKI's[1] PEACE DECLARATION

(1990–1975)

Peace Declaration (1990)

【Comments by the City of Hiroshima】
〈Praise and hopes for nuclear disarmament; making the "three non-nuclear principles" into law; denuclearization of the Asia-Pacific region; first mention of support for non-Japanese A-bomb survivors〉

A summer day, a solitary bomb, a single instant; and Hiroshima was transformed into a raging inferno[2] and a hell on earth.

Countless precious lives were tragically lost, and even those who somehow managed to survive have lived in constant fear of radioactivity's grim after-effects.

Over the last 45 years, Hiroshima has risen from the agony of its bombing and, firm in the determination that the evil never be repeated, has constantly pressed for lasting world peace and called for the abolition of nuclear weapons and the renunciation[3] of war. Today, Hiroshima's prayer has become the world's prayer.

The long history of distrust and discord is drawing to

---

1) 荒木武(市長任期1975年2月〜1991年2月)　2) [名]地獄、業火　3) [名]拒否、否定

a close, and there are finally signs of a new era of trust and cooperation.

Long the symbol of East-West discord, even the Berlin Wall has come down, the Cold War structures are fated to end, the quest is on for a new world order of peace, and mankind is taking the first steps toward altering its history.

The leaders of the United States and the Soviet Union concurred[4] this June on the first real reduction ever in their nuclear arsenals, and agreement has been reached on negotiating further nuclear disarmament. Protocols have also been signed toward the abolition of chemical weapons and there is promise of an early agreement on reductions in conventional forces[5] as well. Hiroshima has the highest regard for this tide of disarmament changing the fate of mankind from one of annihilation to one of survival. All of the nuclear powers should heed this global call and move immediately to ban all nuclear tests and to abolish nuclear weapons, and all countries everywhere should make greater efforts for total disarmament across the board.

In line with the relaxation of world tensions, it is incumbent upon the government of Japan, in keeping with the pacifist ideals underpinning[6] its Constitution, to curtail[7] military spending, to pass the three non-nuclear principles into law so as to prevent the mooting[8] of these national tenets[9], and to take the initiative in making the Asia-Pacific region a nuclear-free zone of disarmament, as well as to undertake vigorous

---

4) concur on~ ～において合意する　5) conventional forces 通常戦力
6) underpin［他動］支える、土台を補強する　7) curtail［他動］削減する
8) moot［他動］議題にのせる　9) national tenets 国是

diplomatic efforts for the building of a world order of peace.

This March, the renovation of the Atomic Bomb Dome was completed with the generous contributions and the fervent wishes for peace from all over the world. Annual admissions to the Peace Memorial Museum topped 1.5 million last year. And the number of cities sympathizing with the Program to Promote the Solidarity of Cities towards the Total Abolition of Nuclear Weapons[10] has grown to 287 cities in 50 countries worldwide. All of this is testimony to the depths of the popular longing for peace.

Today, we will host the 1990 Women's International Peace Symposium in Hiroshima with its vigorous discussions of what women can do to bring about peace and the abolition of nuclear weapons.

Hiroshima will continue to lay the grim realities of nuclear attack before the world, and we are promoting the establishment here of an international peace research institute to make the world more aware of the need for nuclear disarmament.

Hiroshima renews its appeal:

For an immediate and complete end to nuclear testing and the abolition of nuclear arms.

For the United States, the Soviet Union, and the other nuclear countries to reveal the full truth of the harm caused by their obstinate nuclear testing over the last forty-plus years and to promptly implement restitution measures for the environment and the people.

---

10) Program to Promote the Solidarity of Cities towards the Total Abolition of Nuclear Weapons 核兵器廃絶を求める世界平和都市連帯推進計画

For the world leaders and those young people who will guide future generations to visit Hiroshima and to see for themselves the horror of nuclear war.

Hiroshima's heart also goes out to all of the oppressed people everywhere who are victims of starvation, poverty, the suppression of human rights, refugee status, regional conflicts, global environmental devastation, and other problems, and we earnestly hope that the international community will cooperate for the earliest possible solution of these problems.

Today, in this Peace Memorial Ceremony to commemorate the 45th anniversary of the atomic bombing of Hiroshima, we express our heartfelt condolences to all of the victims of that bombing. We strongly appeal to the government of Japan to use the Survey of Atomic Bomb Victims in promptly instituting a systematic program of support for the *hibakusha* grounded upon the principle of national indemnification. At the same time, we earnestly hope that positive efforts will be made to promote support for those *hibakusha* resident on the Korean Peninsula, in the United States, and elsewhere, and we rededicate ourselves to the cause of peace.

*   *   *

Peace Declaration (1989)

【A comment by the City of Hiroshima】
〈The Third World Conference of Mayors for Peace through Inter-city Solidarity〉

"Let all the souls here rest in peace; for we shall not repeat the evil." Having experienced the nuclear hellfire, Hiroshima has continued to warn incessantly that, as stated in this epitaph, nuclear weapons are incompatible with human existence.

The voice of Hiroshima having aroused world opinion, we see the first fetal stirrings[11] toward a vast human movement in the direction of abolishing nuclear weapons and achieving lasting peace.

Building upon the Intermediate Nuclear Forces treaty[12], the United States and the Soviet Union are now negotiating for reductions in their strategic nuclear forces[13]. Disarmament proposals have also been made on short-range nuclear forces and on conventional forces. Underlying these developments is the historical groundswell of worldwide support for disarmament. The cold-war framework of East-West relations structured around relations between the United States and the Soviet Union is beginning to crumble[14] after having defined postwar politics for so long, and the world is groping its way toward a new order of international peace. It is imperative that we seize the moment to build a brighter future for all humankind.

---

11) fetal stirrings 胎動   12) Intermediate Nuclear Forces treaty 中距離核戦力全廃条約   13) strategic nuclear forces 戦略核兵器   14) crumble[自動]崩壊する

The government of Japan should return to the pacifist ideals embodied in its Constitution and, rather than resisting the current of detente, should curb its military spending and take the initiative in working for lasting world peace. It is of paramount[15] importance that Japan exercise vigorous diplomatic efforts for peace, gaining the cooperation of the other countries concerned and working for the non-nuclearization of the Asia-Pacific region. Along with making every effort to discover the truth about the nuclear-armed U.S. military aircraft that sank off Okinawa, it is imperative that the government establish policies to keep the three non-nuclear principles from becoming moot and urge the United States government in the strongest terms to strictly observe these basic tenets of national policy.

This year marks the centennial of Hiroshima's incorporation as a city and the fortieth anniversary of the passage of the Hiroshima Peace Memorial City Construction Law. Significantly, Hiroshima is currently hosting the Second World Conference of Mayors for Peace through Inter-city Solidarity. Bringing together about 130 mayors from more than 30 countries, this Conference transcends systemic differences and national borders to engage in vigorous discussion of The Role of Cities in the Nuclear Age: Toward the Total Abolition of Nuclear Weapons.

In October, the Ninth World Congress of the International Physicians for the Prevention of Nuclear War[16] will be held in Hiroshima around the basic

---

15) ［形］最高の ※paramount importance 最重要 16) World Congress of the International Physicians for the Pre-vention of Nuclear War 核戦争防止国際医師会議

theme of No More Hiroshimas: An Eternal Commitment.

The United Nations Special Session on Disarmament was held in Kyoto in April, the first time it has ever met in Japan. The participants in this Special Session visited Hiroshima, saw for themselves the awful aftermath of nuclear weapons, heightened their awareness of this horrible potential, and strengthened their determination to abolish nuclear weapons.

This year's special appeal for funds to preserve the Atomic Bomb Dome and its warning of the danger that nuclear weapons pose to human survival has drawn a strong response from Japan and overseas. Last fiscal year, the Peace Memorial Museum drew over 1.45 million visitors, a record number. These facts are eloquent witness to the way the Spirit of Hiroshima is spreading irresistibly.

Hiroshima must continue to toll[17] its warning at home and abroad until a new world order is established founded upon co-existence and co-prosperity[18] for all humankind.

Profoundly sympathetic to the suffering of all the people of the world, our hearts go out to the many people suffering from starvation, destitution[19], abasement[20] of human rights, the destruction of the global environment, and other wrongs, and Hiroshima appeals fervently to all countries concerned for a prompt resolution of these ills.

Hiroshima continues to issue its appeal:

---

17) toll［他動］（鐘を鳴らして）知らせる　※toll its warning　警鐘を打ち鳴らす
18) co-existence and co-prosperity 共存共栄　19)［名］貧困　20)［名］屈辱、汚辱

For a prompt and comprehensive nuclear test ban and the abolition of all such weapons.

For all of the leaders of today and tomorrow alike to visit Hiroshima and to see for themselves the truth of nuclear destruction.

For the establishment of an international research institute in Hiroshima devoted to peace and disarmament.

Today, on the occasion of the 44th Peace Memorial Ceremony, we offer our heartfelt prayers for the repose of the souls of the many victims of the atomic bombing. Along with appealing most strongly to the government of Japan to institute policies to support relief for the aging *hibakusha* under the principle of national indemnification, we do hereby pledge our every and undying effort to the cause of world peace.

* * *

Peace Declaration (1988)

[A comment by the City of Hiroshima]
⟨Results of the Third Special Session of the UN General Assembly on Disarmament⟩

Hiroshima. The very name is symbolic of mankind's fervent quest for the abolition of nuclear weapons and the attainment of lasting peace.

That blazing holocaust of 43 years ago even today

remains burned into our memories. "No More Hiroshimas." This is the anguished[21] cry of all people subjected to the horrible nuclear threat.

Hiroshima's appeal has today spread worldwide, and public opinion around the globe is pressing to transform international politics from conflict to dialogue, from distrust to friendship.

The recent signing of the INF Treaty between the United States and the Soviet Union gives hope for a future dominated not by the threat of annihilation but by the promise of survival, and it is a worthwhile historical first step toward comprehensive nuclear disarmament. Yet the numbers involved are small, and we must not forget the fact that not only land masses but also the seas and even space are all arenas for modern nuclear strategy.

It was in this context that the Third Special Session of the United Nations General Assembly Devoted to Disarmament was held and that I made the strongest possible presentation of the Hiroshima Spirit of yearning for lasting peace. Several Vice Presidents from the World Conference of Mayors for Peace through Inter-city Solidarity also attended this Special Session with me. Today, the Program to Promote Solidarity of Cities towards the Total Abolition of Nuclear Weapons includes 228 municipalities in 40 countries and is steadily growing, becoming a new force for coalescing[22] world opinion for the abolition of all nuclear weapons.

It is most regrettable that representatives more

---

21) [形] 苦悩に満ちた   22) coalesce [自動] 一つになる

concerned with narrow national interests prevented the Special Session from adopting a final resolution calling for comprehensive global disarmament - this despite the fact that it drew the participation of a record number of government leaders and non-governmental organization representatives and despite the animated debate that took place on the specifics of a nuclear test ban and nuclear non-proliferation.

Yet the voice of Hiroshima rings out. The abolition of nuclear weapons is the number-one priority issue for human survival, and there must be no digression from[23] this goal. Just as we are calling upon all nations to strengthen and revitalize the United Nations' peacekeeping functions, so do we hope that the United Nations will take the initiative in holding an international conference on peace and disarmament here at Hiroshima's ground zero.

Today, Hiroshima is host to the '88 International Youth Peace Symposium in Hiroshima enabling young people from sister cities worldwide to sit down and talk with the people of Hiroshima to ensure that the Hiroshima experience is not forgotten. Next August, the Second World Conference of Mayors for Peace through Inter-city Solidarity will be held in both Hiroshima and Nagasaki to further strengthen the bonds of solidarity. And in October 1989, the Ninth Congress of the International Physicians for the Prevention of Nuclear War will be held in Hiroshima to renew its resolve that there be No More Hiroshimas.

---

23) digression from~ ～からの脱線

Hiroshima is determined to continue to sound the alarm and to arouse world opinion in the cause of world peace so that there is infinite potential for a bright future for all mankind in the 21st century.

Hiroshima renews its appeal: For a comprehensive nuclear test ban. For the total abolition of all nuclear weapons. For present and future world leaders to come to Hiroshima and see for themselves the devastating horror of nuclear war. For the establishment of an international research institute for peace and disarmament in Hiroshima.

Hiroshima is also deeply concerned about the millions of people suffering from starvation, impoverishment, human rights abuses, regional conflicts, and other forms of deprivation[24], and we appeal urgently to all nations to find a just resolution to these people's desperate plight.

The government of Japan should actively pursue measures to contribute to world peace in keeping with the modem significance of the Constitution's ideal of peace and in line with its three non-nuclear principles. In addition, we most strongly appeal to the government to promptly implement *hibakusha* relief measures in the spirit of national indemnification.

Today - the 43rd anniversary of that fateful August 6 so many years ago - we offer our prayers for the repose of the victims' souls and pledge ourselves to working untiringly for the cause of lasting world peace.

---

24) [名] (必需品の) 欠乏、貧困

Peace Declaration (1987)

【Comments by the City of Hiroshima】
〈The 10th anniversary of UN Disarmament week; expectations for the Third Special Session of the UN General Assembly on Disarmament to be held during the coming year〉

A City of International Peace and Culture reborn from the catastrophe of the atomic bombing, Hiroshima has dedicated itself to appealing for the total abolition of nuclear weapons and for coexistence and co-prosperity for all peoples everywhere. Today marks the forty-second anniversary of that fateful day.

"Let all the souls here rest in peace; For we shall not repeat the evil." So reads the epitaph on the Memorial Cenotaph, embodying a mournful prayer for the victims of this tragedy as well as a solemn pledge and sacred commandment[25] to all peoples past, present, and future. Renewing our commitment, we must strive untiringly in our efforts to ensure that this Hiroshima Spirit is observed worldwide.

Among the commemorative events being held today is a symposium with leading journalists from the nuclear powers in an attempt to turn the weight of world opinion toward the total elimination of all nuclear weapons. In 1989, the World Conference of Mayors for Peace through Inter-city Solidarity will again be held in Hiroshima and Nagasaki to broaden

---

25) [名]戒律、命令

the bonds of friendship among cities and citizens everywhere. In the same year, International Physicians for the Prevention of Nuclear War will hold its World Congress in Hiroshima to further the quest for a safe, nuclear-free world.

It is increasingly important that future generations be told about the horrors of nuclear war. It is thus most encouraging that over five million schoolchildren have visited Hiroshima over the last ten years, seeing with their own eyes the truth of this bombing and learning in their own hearts the luxury and fragility of life.

As the nuclear arms race expands into space and the world continues to be possessed by power politics and the balance of terror, it becomes increasingly likely that all life will be snuffed out. This is a truly intolerable situation.

In this nuclear age, it is imperative that we bring together mankind's collective wisdom and move from distrust to dialogue, from fear to friendship, in overcoming national interests and embarking on[26] a new path that will lead to lasting world peace.

The recent East-West agreement toward the abolition of intermediate-range nuclear forces is thus a success for the broad-based international public opposition to nuclear weapons, and Hiroshima is watching these negotiations with utmost interest.

Starvation, refugee dislocation, and human rights oppression[27] are among the other urgent problems demanding solution.

---

26) embark on~ ～に乗り出す　27) [名]抑圧、圧制

This year is the tenth year since the United Nations Disarmament Week was first declared, and the Third Special Session of the United Nations General Assembly on Disarmament will be held next year - we devoutly hope most successfully.

Hiroshima reiterates its appeal: Let the nuclear powers immediately institute a complete ban on testing ; let the United States and the Soviet Union convene a Summit Meeting for the early conclusion of a comprehensive nuclear disarmament treaty ; and let all the world's leaders come to Hiroshima so that they may affirm for themselves the reality of nuclear war.

Representing the only country to have been atomic-bombed in war, the government of Japan should embark upon the diplomacy of peace more vigorously and take a greater initiative for the abolition of nuclear weapons in line with its Constitutional ideals of peace and in firm adherence to its three non-nuclear principles.

At this Peace Memorial Ceremony commemorating those unforgettable events of forty-two years ago, we offer our sincere prayers for the repose of the bomb's many victims. Appealing to the government of Japan to move quickly to establish enhanced compassionate policy measures for the relief of aging *hibakusha* (atomic bomb survivors) and bereaved families[28] alike under the principle of national indemnification, we do here pledge ourselves to work untiringly for the cause of peace so that this evil never be repeated.

---

28) bereaved families 遺族

* * *

Peace Declaration (1986)

【Comments by the City of Hiroshima】
〈Chernobyl Nuclear Power Plant accident in the Soviet Union; human rights suppression issues〉

Peace. That is the fervent prayer of the people of Hiroshima.

Forty-one years ago, on August 6, 1945, Hiroshima was devastated by a scorching flash of light and an earth-shaking explosion. The streets were massed with people, many of them dead almost instantly, and many of the rest wondering if death was not the kinder fate. It was truly an earthly inferno surpassing imagination.

Risen from its ruins like the mythical phoenix. Hiroshima has repeatedly appealed for the total abolition of nuclear weapons and the creation of lasting world peace so that the evil not be repeated.

For a brief interlude[29] beginning last August 6, a new age of nuclear disarmament appeared to be dawning as the Soviet Union announced a moratorium on nuclear testing and summit talks between the United States and the Soviet Union were resumed. However, little progress has been made in these nuclear disarmament negotiations. Instead, the world's nuclear arsenals continue unabated[30] their quantitative and qualitative expansion, accompanied now by a dangerous new

29) [名]幕間、合間 30) [形]衰えない

nuclear strategy that would extend the risk of atomic bomb holocaust into space.

The Soviet nuclear accident at Chernobyl brought the people of the world face to face with the horrors of lethal[31] radioactivity, arousing serious concern about the lack of mechanisms for international controls and cooperation in case of a nuclear power plant accident. The world shuddered[32] as it witnessed the reality of our nuclear age - the ease with which a nuclear disaster in one country can spill its deadly contamination and consequences into other countries.

Compounding this, regional conflicts and terrorism have become increasingly commonplace, and peace suffers from the growing specter of starvation, the plight of refugees worldwide, the denial of human rights, and other affronts to human decency.

Not long before he was so tragically felled by an assassin's bullet, Sweden's Prime Minister Olof Palme visited the Hiroshima Peace Memorial Museum. Seeing the human shadow imprinted on the stone steps by the scorching heat of the atomic bomb, he remarked apocalyptically[33] that a nuclear war now would probably erase even the shadows on the stones.

When the members of the Nobel Peace Prize-winning International Physicians for the Prevention of Nuclear War visited Hiroshima this June, they were aghast[34] at the historical record and moved to issue a vigorous appeal for an immediate halt to all nuclear testing.

Today, Hiroshima Day is being observed in cities and

31)［形］致命的な、死を招く　32) shudder［自動］震える、ぞっとする　33)［副］予言的に、黙示的に　34) be aghast at~　~に驚愕する

towns around the world. In Mexico, for example, the heads of state and government of six non-aligned nations[35] are meeting together to appeal for nuclear disarmament.

Calling for the total abolition of all nuclear weapons and the attainment of world peace, the voice of Hiroshima is today the voice of all peoples everywhere.

There is no time to lose.

The nuclear powers should immediately and permanently halt all nuclear tests. Holding the fate of all humankind in their hands, the United States and the Soviet Union should hold a summit meeting in Hiroshima City-both victim and survivor of the world's first atomic bombing-and take the first practical steps toward nuclear disarmament.

We strongly and respectfully request the Secretary-General of the United Nations to urge the leaders of the United States and the Soviet Union to visit Hiroshima, and we further request the Secretary-General to take immediate action to convene the Third Special Session of the United Nations General Assembly Devoted to Disarmament.

In keeping with the ideals of peace embodied in the Constitution and steadfastly adhering to[36] the three non-nuclear principles, the people and government of Japan should take the initiative in leading efforts for the elimination of nuclear weapons and the attainment of world peace.

This year has been designated the International Year

---

35) non-aligned nations 非同盟諸国   36) adhere to~ ~に固執する

of Peace.

We are holding this Peace Summit in Hiroshima today to mobilize the world's conscience for the total abolition of nuclear weapons and the attainment of lasting world peace.

Hiroshima repeats its appeal.

It is essential that all cities and citizens of the world join together in expanding the circle of solidarity transcending national boundaries, partisan ideologies, and religious creeds[37] to strengthen the bonds of human friendship and solidarity.

Today, on the occasion of this ceremony marking the forty-first anniversary of the atomic bombing of Hiroshima, we offer our prayer for the repose of the victims' souls, request that the government of Japan enhance its relief measures for survivors and bereaved families alike under the principle of national indemnification, and rededicate ourselves anew to the cause of peace.

*   *   *

Peace Declaration (1985)

【Comments by the City of Hiroshima】
〈Holding the World Conference of Mayors for Peace through Inter-city Solidarity; hopes for youth during the International Youth Year〉

---

37) [名]教義、(宗教上の) 信条

No more Hiroshimas.

It was forty years ago today during the hot summer that the heat waves, fiery blast, and radiation emitted by the first nuclear weapon ever used against a human target burned all living things in a blinding flash and turned the city of Hiroshima into a plain of scorched rubble.

Standing in the ruins, we, the citizens of Hiroshima, foresaw that any war fought with nuclear weapons would mean the annihilation of humanity and the end of civilization - and we have consistently appealed to the world for the total abolition of nuclear weapons.

Despite these untiring efforts, more and more nuclear weapons have been produced; they have been made more and more sophisticated[38]; and they have been deployed ready for strategic and tactical use[39]. Humankind continues to face the threat of nuclear annihilation.

Although the nuclear superpowers, the United States and the Soviet Union, finally resumed their long-suspended negotiations on nuclear disarmament this March, the talks have made deplorably[40] little progress as the superpowers use the facade of negotiation to jockey for advantage while they expand the nuclear arms race into outer space.

Today's hesitation leads to tomorrow's destruction.

In order that Hiroshima's inferno never be repeated anywhere, we strongly urge the United States and the Soviet Union, who hold the fate of humankind in their

38) [形]非常に高度な   39) strategic and tactical use 戦略的かつ戦術的使
用   40) [副]遺憾ながら

hands, to halt all nuclear testing immediately and to take decisive steps at the summit talks in Geneva toward the total abolition of nuclear weapons in the interests of all humankind.

As the only country to have experienced nuclear devastation, Japan and the government of Japan should steadfastly adhere to its three non-nuclear principles policy and should take the initiative in seeking the elimination of nuclear weapons. A census of A-bomb victims is being conducted this year, and it is our sincere hope that all due measures will be taken to mitigate the suffering of A-bomb survivors on the basis of the principle of national indemnity, taking into consideration the distinctive characteristics of ailments[41] induced by atomic bombing.

Along with these efforts, Hiroshima, an A-bombed city, has been devoting itself to building a city dedicated to peace - a living symbol of the ideal of lasting world peace. It is in this spirit that we are hosting the First World Conference of Mayors for Peace through Inter-city Solidarity this year, for it is our hope that all the cities of the world aspiring to lasting peace will be able to develop inter-city solidarity transcending national boundaries, ideologies and creeds and will impart added momentum to the international quest for peace.

This year also marks the International Youth Year. We hope that the young people of the world - the leaders of the twenty-first century - will inherit the Spirit of Hiroshima, strengthen friendship and solidarity among

---

41) [名]慢性的な病気

themselves, and exert their utmost efforts in the cause of peace.

The fates of all of us are bound together here on earth. There can be no survival for any without peaceful co-existence for all. Humankind has no future if that future does not include co-prosperity. In order to save this verdant[42] planet from the grim death of nuclear winter, we must draw upon our common wisdom in overcoming distrust and confrontation. Sharing our planet's finite resources in the spirit of mutual understanding and cooperation, we must eliminate starvation and poverty.

No more Hiroshimas.

We must strengthen the bonds of friendship and solidarity among all peoples so as to save the world from the evil of war.

Today, on the occasion of the fortieth anniversary of the atomic bombing of Hiroshima, we pray for the souls of the A-bomb victims and rededicate our lives to the eradication of nuclear weapons and the pursuit of lasting peace.

*　　*　　*

Peace Declaration (1984)

August 6, 1945. Who can forget that momentous flash of light when the atomic bomb exploded above Hiroshima, that terrible heat, and that earthshaking explosion!

---

42) [形] 緑に覆われた

Reborn out of the indescribable catastrophe of atomic bombing, Hiroshima has repeatedly appealed for the abolition of nuclear arms and the attainment of lasting peace.

Yet the distrust and hostility between the United States and the Soviet Union festers[43] unabated, and the two superpowers seek an artificial security in the doctrine[44] of nuclear deterrence and ever greater stocks of nuclear weapons. Having broken off their Strategic Arms Reduction Talks[45] and their Intermediate-range Nuclear Forces negotiations, they pursue a reckless nuclear arms race toward oblivion[46].

Not content with deploying sophisticated intermediate-range missiles in Europe and Asia, they now project their nuclear strategies even into space, thus exacerbating global military tensions and pushing the world to the very brink of nuclear war.

Nuclear war will leave neither winners nor losers, for all humankind will perish in its holocaust.

Confronted with this danger, there is a global welling up of movements for disarmament, including the initiative by the leaders of India, Sweden, and four other countries calling on the nuclear powers for nuclear disarmament.

Popular campaigns against nuclear arms have arisen spontaneously, and "the Spirit of Hiroshima" has permeated the whole world to strengthen the groundswell of international public opinion in the cause of peace.

We solemnly urge the nuclear powers to heed this

---

43) fester［自動］悪化する、(怒りなどが) 募る　44) ［名］理論、主義　45) Strategic Arms Reduction Talks 戦略兵器削減交渉　46) ［名］忘却

international outcry[47], to initiate an immediate and comprehensive nuclear test ban, and to begin to eliminate their nuclear armories. We especially urge the United States and the Soviet Union, which together have the power of life of death over our species, to promptly resume their disarmament negotiations, to overcome the discord between them, and to hold a Peace Summit.

As the only country ever to have been subjected to nuclear bombings, Japan should adhere fast to its Constitutional principles of peace, faithfully uphold its three non-nuclear principles, and do its utmost to promote nuclear disarmament and the easing of East-West tensions.

We are today at an important crossroad, one path leading to survival and the other to death and destruction.

It is imperative that we uphold the lofty ideal of lasting world peace and use our collective wisdom to redirect the tide of history from confrontation to communication, from animosity[48] to amiability[49].

Hiroshima and Nagasaki have appealed for solidarity among all cities everywhere desiring peace, cooperation, and the abolition of the nuclear threat. This appeal has found an increasingly receptive audience, and we now propose to hold a "World Conference of Mayors for Peace through Inter-city Solidarity" next year on the 40th anniversary of the atomic bombing to see if a new order of peace cannot be born of this inter-city

---

47) [名]抗議　48) [名]敵意　49) [名]友好

solidarity.

Today on the occasion of the 39th anniversary of the atomic bombing, we call upon the Government of Japan to promote and strengthen relief measures for atomic bomb survivors and bereaved families under the principle of national indemnification - just as we pray for the repose of the souls of the fallen victims and pledge ourselves anew to the cause of peace.

*   *   *

Peace Declaration (1983)

【A comment by the City of Hiroshima】
〈Hiroshima and Nagasaki mayors' promotion of the Program to Promote Solidarity of Cities Towards the Total Abolition of Nuclear Weapons〉

It is now thirty-eight years since that tragic day. Haunted by intense anxiety and revulsion[50] at the nuclear arms race, Hiroshima once again finds itself under a hot August sun.

In spite of repeated talks on disarmament, the nuclear arms race, with the Unites States and the Soviet Union in the forefront, continues it appalling[51] acceleration. Under the increasing menace[52] of nuclear arms, humanity is confronted with the danger of annihilation, as demonstrated by the deployment of SS 20 nuclear missiles and the planned deployment of Pershing II

---

50) [名]嫌悪   51) [形]凄まじい、甚だしい   52) [名]脅威

nuclear missiles in Europe and the build-up of nuclear weapons taking place in the Far East.

In this tense situation, however, campaigns against nuclear weapons have arisen spontaneously. With voices calling out, "Do not repeat the tragedy of Hiroshima," and "No More Hiroshimas," the anti-nuclear weapons movement is gaining international attention.

As a part of the World Disarmament Campaign adopted at the Second Special Session on Disarmament, the United Nations will dispatch the first special delegation on disarmament to Hiroshima this autumn and a permanent exhibit on atomic bomb destruction is planned at the U.N. Headquarters. The United Nations has thus started to make new efforts towards educating world opinion, particularly future generations in perpetuity on the reality of disaster of the atomic bomb.

In January 1983, the mayors of Hiroshima and Nagasaki made an appeal entitled "Program to Promote Solidarity of Cities Towards the Total Abolition of Nuclear Weapons." This growing solidarity is spreading beyond national boundaries, with messages of fervent support coming from all parts of the world.

It is high time that people in all countries depart from their history of hostility, be aware of human dignity, communicate more deeply with each other, and build bonds of trust and goodwill.

Today's hesitation leads to tomorrow's destruction.

In order to halt the ever-expanding nuclear arms race, we urge the nuclear powers, above all else, to immediately conclude a "Comprehensive Nuclear-Weapons-Test Ban Treaty," to stop the production and deployment of all nuclear arms, and to abolish all nuclear arms completely.

We especially urge the superpowers, the United States and Soviet Union, to hold a Peace Summit, to rise above their military and strategic considerations, and, with a global citizens' perspective, to make a decision that shall bring hope to the world.

Japan, the only country that has experienced the atomic bomb, maintains the three non-nuclear principles on the basis of its peace-centered Constitution, and is expected to take the initiative in promoting the Peace Summit between the United States and the Soviet Union and, thus, to be a beacon for world peace.

Today, on the occasion of this ceremony, we pray for the repose of the souls of the victims of the atomic bomb, and firmly pledge ourselves to carrying out relief measures on the basis of national indemnity for the atomic bomb survivors, to the total abolition of nuclear weapons, and to general and complete disarmament.

* * *

Peace Declaration (1982)

【A comment by the City of Hiroshima】
⟨Report on the mayor's appeal to the UN Special Session, proposal for city solidarity and establishing an international institute for research on peace in Hiroshima⟩

One torch ignites another, in unending succession, and still the first torch keeps burning. Thus the 'spirit of Hiroshima', dedicated to peace, should be shared by all people and handed down to posterity.

The devastation of Hiroshima on that day was an omen[53] of the advent[54] of dark clouds threatening the prospects for the survival of the human race. Having experienced the reality of that threat, Hiroshima has appealed to the world unceasingly for the total abolition of nuclear weapons and for general and complete disarmament.

Yet the nations - with the United States and the Soviet Union in the forefront - continue locked in confrontation. While nuclear weapons steadily proliferate in quantity, doctrines of limited nuclear war and preemptive nuclear attack[55] arise. The human race is now faced with the very great danger of an outbreak of nuclear war.

When Dr. Olof Palme, Chairman of the Independent Commission on Disarmament and Security Issues, and Mr. Sandro Pertini, President of the Republic of Italy,

53) [名]兆し   54) [名]出現、到来   55) preemptive nuclear attack 先制核攻撃

came to Hiroshima, they were horrified to witness the cruelty of the atomic disaster. They expressed their profound fear that there could be neither winner nor loser in a nuclear war.

The governments of nations should seriously consider the unavoidable[56] fact that an aspiration[57] towards the abolition of nuclear arms is growing universally, everywhere in the world. They must not lose a moment in promoting disarmament, and in quickening their pace on the road towards peace.

Critical as this world situation clearly is, the Second Special Session of the United Nations General Assembly devoted to disarmament - to our profound regret - did not reach any agreement on the "Comprehensive Disarmament Programme[58]", for the member states were unable to overcome the barrier of mutual distrust among themselves.

However, the resolution of the First Special Session that the prevention of nuclear war and nuclear disarmament be given the highest priority was reconfirmed by the Second Special Session. Furthermore, agreement was newly reached on launching the "World Disarmament Campaign" with the aim of forming a consensus towards disarmament, and on accepting the Japanese Government's proposal that special research fellows in disarmament should be dispatched to Hiroshima and Nagasaki.

At the Second Special Session the Mayor of Hiroshima offered his testimony of the Hiroshima catastrophe,

56) [形]避けられない、不可避の 57) [名]熱望 58) Comprehensive Disarmament Programme 包括的軍縮計画

and appealed for the attainment of the city's aspirations towards peace.

We here repeat the same appeal.

We call most urgently for the immediate and complete banning of nuclear tests, and the freezing of all nuclear weapons stocks, which should ultimately be eradicated.

We also call for the solidarity of cities throughout the world which share a common cause with Hiroshima.

Furthermore, we propose (1) that the leaders of the nuclear powers and other nations should visit Hiroshima to confirm the true nature of the disaster of the atomic bombing; (2) that a Summit Conference on disarmament should be held in Hiroshima; and (3) that an international institute for research on peace and disarmament should be established in Hiroshima.

Hiroshima is not merely a witness of history.

Hiroshima is an everlasting warning for the future of mankind.

If Hiroshima is ever forgotten, it is evident that the evil will be repeated and human history be brought to an end.

Today, on the occasion of the 37th anniversary of the atomic bombing, we devoutly pray for the repose of the souls of the fallen victims. We call urgently on the Japanese Government to promote and strengthen - on the basis of a national indemnity - the relief measures for the atomic bomb survivors still suffering both physically and mentally, and for the bereaved families.

Hiroshima commits itself to continuing the appeal to

the world for peace while keeping the torch of peace aflame.

* * *

Peace Declaration (1981)

【A comment by the City of Hiroshima】
〈First mention of the "three non-nuclear principles"〉

"Let all the souls here rest in peace; For we shall not repeat the evil." These words compose the pledge we have dedicated to the A-bomb victims. In it, we also appeal for the abolition of nuclear weapons and the renunciation of war.

However, the nuclear powers, with the United States and the Soviet Union in the forefront, continue an ever-expanding arms race which serves only to strengthen their rivalry. Consequently, mankind today is confronted with the real possibility of self-extinction.

Pope John Paul II[59], comprehending this danger and potential tragedy, stood on this very spot last February and made an appeal to the entire world. He observed that to remember the past is to commit oneself to the future. In particular, he emphasized that to remember Hiroshima is to abhor[60] nuclear war and to commit oneself to peace. Above all, Pope John Paul II stressed that peace always must be pursued and protected.

In spite of the common sense of such appeals, nuclear

59) Pope John Paul II ローマ教皇ヨハネ・パウロ二世　60) abhor[他動]ひどく嫌悪する

weapons are becoming increasingly sophisticated and diversified. They are ready to be deployed on the ground, in the air and at sea. Such weapons, ready at any time, lead to dangerous confrontations between nations. They possess unbelievable powers of destruction, powers estimated to be approximately one-and-one-half million times as great as the atomic bomb dropped on Hiroshima. Thus, each and every day, we all are threatened by this "Balance of Terror." This danger is aggravated by the increasing possibility of one side mounting a preemptive strike against the other in an attempt to break this precarious[61] balance. It is obvious that when a nuclear war begins, no one will survive.

The possession of nuclear weapons can no longer guarantee the security of the human race. Only total nuclear disarmament can guarantee security and thus pave the way for peace. We must recognize this truth.

Thus it is time for all of us to look at this issue from a global viewpoint, giving the highest priority to the survival of the human race. Only then will it be possible to overcome confrontations between ideas, creeds, and political systems and build a path towards a peace based on cooperation and interdependence.

In the forthcoming Second Special Session of the United Nations General Assembly devoted to Disarmament, all Member States should show the deepest respect for this spirit. On the initiative of the nuclear powers, a specific agreement should be reached

---

61) [形] 不安定な、危ない

which will lead to the total abolition of nuclear weapons and eventual complete disarmament. For example, a prohibition on the use of nuclear arms, expansion of the nuclear-free zone and a total ban on nuclear tests are measures that should be carried out immediately. As citizens of a peace-loving nation we sincerely hope that our government will take the lead in these peace efforts, while maintaining its commitment to the three anti-nuclear principles.

Today, on August sixth, the thirty-sixth anniversary of the atomic bombing, we, the citizens of Hiroshima, pray devoutly in tribute to the souls of the A-bomb victims. We are, more than ever, fully aware of our responsibility and devotion to peace. We express our desire for expanded and strengthened relief measures for survivors and their bereaved families on the basis of national indemnity. Thus, we hereby make a strong appeal to the whole world to continue to work for peace.

*   *   *

Peace Declaration (1980)

【Comments by the City of Hiroshima】
〈Regret for the problem of refugees from the Middle East and Southeast Asia; hopes for the enactment of the A-bomb Victims' Relief Law〉

Change brings change inexorably, and nothing stands still - thirty-five years have now passed since that day of disaster.

On that day, Hiroshima took the brunt of the age of nuclear war, in an infernal and scorching blast. Since that day, she has been ever calling for an end to nuclear weapons, praying for a lasting peace for man.

The world situation, at the present time, deeply troubles Hiroshima. World military expenditure has finally come to exceed one billion dollars per day. Its ever-rising curve affects developing countries, and hastens their armament.

Each element in the conflicts in the Middle East and Southeast Asia bears with it the possibility of a development into total nuclear war, even though this depends on the major powers' political strategies. The massive flow of refugees in these regions casts its dark shadow on us.

Apprehension[62] about nuclear expansion and proliferation, and attempts to save mankind from annihilating itself, have been evident in the Limited Test Ban Treaty[63], the Treaty on the Non-Proliferation of Nuclear Weapons, the Strategic Arms Limitation Talks[64] between the United States and the Soviet Union, and other concrete results. In particular, in the first-ever Special Session of the United Nations General Assembly devoted to Disarmament, the member nations reached agreement on the principle that the security of a nation should be maintained not by

---

62) ［名］懸念、不安   63) Limited Test Ban Treaty 部分的核実験禁止条約
64) Strategic Arms Limitation Talks 戦略兵器制限交渉

armament but by disarmament. They resolved at the same time that the reduction of nuclear weapons should be given the highest priority in disarmament issues, with the ultimate aim of abolishing nuclear weapons entirely.

This year, a Peace Memorial Exhibition was held at the United States Senate Office Building, focusing on Hiroshima and Nagasaki. It is clear that international concern about the atomic disaster experience of Hiroshima has been growing. We have little doubt that it will usher in a movement not only to prevent any future victims from being exposed to the horrors of nuclear radiation, but to form an international consensus for the complete eradication of nuclear weapons.

But when we take into account the present realities of the international situation, we see that it will be impossible for us to reach the distant shore of peace, unless we conquer intergovernmental distrust, deep-rooted in the folly of the arms race. Hiroshima therefore now proposes that, before the opening of the second Special Session of the U.N. General Assembly devoted to Disarmament, there should be a World Summit Conference on Peace, with the participation of the leaders of the United States and the Soviet Union. The Government of Japan should take the initiative in advocating this, since, at the first Special Session of the U.N. General Assembly devoted to Disarmament, our Government declared her determination to strengthen still further her diplomatic efforts dedicated to peace and based on international cooperation.

It is now high time for us to call for the solidarity of all mankind, and to shift our common path away from self-destruction towards survival.

Today, on the occasion of the thirty-fifth anniversary of the atomic bombing, we pray devoutly for the repose of the souls of the A-bomb victims; we express our desire for the earliest enactment of the A-bomb victims' relief law, based on the acceptance of national responsibility for indemnity; and we pledge all our efforts to ensure the survival of mankind.

* * *

Peace Declaration (1979)

【Comments by the City of Hiroshima】
〈Problems of radiation exposure; first reference to problems of hunger and poverty; measures to aid A-bomb survivors〉

Hiroshima has the inescapable duty of appealing and campaigning ceaselessly for peace. And ever since that scorching flash of August 6, Hiroshima's deep desire for peace has moved her to call on the peoples of the world again and again for the total abolition of nuclear weapons and the renunciation of war.

So far a number of efforts for the cause of peace have

been made at the international level. The United Nations in particular took an important positive step last year, when it held a Special General Assembly on the question of Disarmament for the first time in its history. This special session urged an historical conversion to the reduction of weapons, aiming at the abolition of nuclear weapons as the ultimate objective. In response to this, the Disarmament Committee has concentrated its combined wisdom on preparations for the next Special General Assembly on Disarmament, to be held three years from now.

Elsewhere, strategic arms limitation talks are now in progress between United States of America and the Union of Soviet Socialist Republics. Immense energy has also been devoted to Middle East peace negotiations.

Nevertheless, in spite of these efforts, the reality of international politics finds some nations still absorbed in boundless arms expansion based on a competition for superior nuclear capability, so that they are acquiring an infinite destructive power.

A series of nuclear tests, carried through so far without any regard for the protests of the people of Hiroshima, has presented the world once more with the problem of global radiation exposure. Thus the fears and warnings of Hiroshima's citizens have turned out to be more than justified.

All nuclear weapons testing should be halted immediately. Not one single human being should be permitted to become a new victim of radiation.

The problems of the A-bomb survivors and of those exposed to nuclear radiation now demand an urgent solution as an international issue.

The Japanese Government has therefore begun consultations to work out a basic structure of thinking on the measures to aid the A-bomb survivors and to re-examine its present measures. We place much of our hope for the future on this effort.

Peace means not only the prevention of war, but also the coexistence and shared prosperity of mankind on a basis of love and reason, transcending the barriers of hatred.

We have to face up to the fact that the nations of the world, in their folly, have wasted the earth's limited resources on the expansion of armaments. By this very process they have hastened the spread of hunger and poverty.

It is now high time for us, on the basis of Hiroshima's unchanging desire for peace, to combine our efforts to alter the current of history towards the construction of a new world, and to lay the foundation of humankind's prosperity.

We pray devoutly for the repose of the souls of the A-bomb victims; and with the same sincerity we pledge all our efforts to an unceasing search for peace, for we believe that the disaster of Hiroshima is an awesome warning to humanity in the nuclear age.

*   *   *

Peace Declaration (1978)

【A comment by the City of Hiroshima】
〈Praise for the UN Special Session on Disarmament〉

In this world, there is nothing more precious than peace.

Based on our tragic atomic bomb experience, we the citizens of Hiroshima, have for more than three decades called for the total abolition of nuclear weapons and the renunciation of war and have consistently been in pursuit of true peace.

This dearest wish of Hiroshima inspired at long last an international conscience to set up the Special Session of the United Nations General Assembly devoted to Disarmament, held in May this year for the first time in its history with 149 Member Nations in attendance.

Representing the citizens of the two cities, the Mayor of Hiroshima, together with the Mayor of Nagasaki, attended the Special Session on Disarmament and also made feasible the epoch-making "Hiroshima-Nagasaki Photographic Exhibit" at the United Nations Headquarters. The photo exhibit vividly reproduced the bare facts of the atomic bomb disasters, rendering great impact upon the visitors to the United Nations, and needless to say, upon the representatives of the Permanent Mission of the United Nations.

In order to achieve the ultimate objective of general and complete disarmament, the nations present at this

Special Session on Disarmament have resolved to establish a new disarmament structure composed of all Member States. This is indeed of great significance.

However, the Nuclear Powers, with the United States and the Soviet Union in the forefront are still conducting nuclear testing, deeply engaged in the development of formidable new types of weapons. Mankind today is confronted with an unprecedented threat of self-extinction arising from the massive accumulation[65] and competitive disposition of the most destructive weapons.

True peace can never be built on the accumulation of weaponry.

The current of international politics, still lingering in perplexity and embedded in mutual distrust between nations, must be changed by the convergence[66] of sound world public opinion surpassing all ideologies.

As a forerunner in peace within the international community, it is now high time that Japan, as the only nation to suffer the atomic bomb catastrophe, should bend her utmost energies in an effort to urge world public opinion, and to aim at the attainment of world-wide consensus for the abolition of nuclear weapons and the renunciation of war.

The people of the world ought to combine their wisdom towards the establishment of a new international order based on the spirit of human coexistence and solidarity, transcending the lines of national boundaries and differences of race. This is the

---

65) [名] 累積、蓄積　66) [名] 結集、集中

only way to build genuine peace - this is the invariable wish of Hiroshima.

Today, on this 33rd Anniversary of the Atomic Bombing when we hold the memorial service for the repose of the souls of the A-bomb victims, I, in the name of all citizens, strongly make this declaration to the whole world.

* * *

Peace Declaration (1977)

【A comment by the City of Hiroshima】
〈Report on the visit of the mayors of Hiroshima and Nagasaki to the UN Headquarters〉

Peace - the spirit of Hiroshima. Hiroshima has been constantly labouring in pursuit of peace.

Nevertheless, the major nuclear powers of the world, with the United States and the Soviet Union in the forefront, are still engaged in a massive armaments race aimed against potential adversaries[67]; they are absorbed in the development of highly technical nuclear weapons, the peak of destructive power has been reached. This is nothing but an act of folly, a blind belief in the dominance of weaponry.

To urge an awakening of conscience and reason, by making known to the world the real facts of the Atomic Bombing, to realize eternal peace by virtue of the

---

67) [名] 敵

abolition of all nuclear weapons, these are the responsibilities imposed upon Hiroshima.

Last year I, as the Mayor of the A-bombed city accompanied the Mayor of Nagasaki on a visit to the United Nations Headquarters. We took with us an ardent wish which had been smouldering[68] over the years in the hearts of our citizens. There we, as survivors, living witnesses, testified the true facts of our atomic bomb experiences, and we strongly appealed for the total abolition of nuclear weapons and the renunciation of war.

To this appeal of ours, both Secretary-General Kurt Waldheim and President H.S. Amerasinghe of the General Assembly, representing the United Nations, respectively emphasized that the sufferings of Hiroshima and Nagasaki are sufferings to be shared by the whole of mankind, and that a new concept of world order should be built from the ashes of Hiroshima and Nagasaki. They deeply sympathized with us, expressing their earnest desire to visit Hiroshima and Nagasaki. His Excellency Amerasinghe is here with us today. His presence means, we hope, that the voice of Hiroshima will be reflected directly in the United Nations. This is of great significance from an international point of view.

The United Nations is scheduled to hold its Special General Assembly on Disarmament sometime in May next year. Great hopes are thus held for its outcome all over the world.

---

68) smoulder[自動]くすぶる

At this very time, we propose that nations throughout the world bind together in perseverance and wisdom toward a final goal: the abolition of nuclear weapons and the renunciation of war, a positive limitation on the world's armaments and an exertion of effort to build a lasting peace, based not on weapons of war, but on international policies which reflect the precious values of our world.

Now, for the people of the world, from the standpoint of all humanity, we must overcome the differences of race and lines of national boundaries and urge world opinion to hasten our strides towards eternal peace.

Today, on the occasion of the 32nd Anniversary of the Atomic Bombing, I, in the name of all citizens, earnestly vow before the souls of the A-bomb fallen victims that we will continue to call strongly for the total abolition of nuclear weapons and to strive vigorously for the realization of eternal peace.

*   *   *

Peace Declaration (1976)

The day has come again, to commemorate the Atomic Bomb Memorial Day.

On this day, at this very time, Hiroshima was annihilated in one instant, and precious lives of countless numbers of people were snatched away. Those who have survived the holocaust find themselves tormented[69] with the physical pain and mental anguish

---

69) torment[他動]苦しめる

caused by radioactive poisoning. Even today thirty-one years after the event, we view with unbearable repentance[70] the passing away of these survivors taking leave of their disease-ridden[71] existence.

We, the citizens of Hiroshima, ever mindful of this cruel experience, clearly foresee the extinction of mankind and an end to civilization should the world drift into a nuclear war. Therefore we have vowed to set aside our griefs and grudges[72] and continuously pleaded before the peoples of the world to abolish weapons and renounce war so that we may "never again repeat the tragedy of Hiroshima."

Nevertheless, the nuclear powers of the world led by the United States of America and the Union of Soviet Socialist Republics have trampled upon[73] the spirit of Hiroshima. Under pretexts of self-defence and world security, these countries have stockpiled huge quantities of nuclear weapons capable of obliterating all mankind. Moreover they have permitted to spread these weapons throughout the world thus acutely increasing the danger of a thermonuclear war[74]. We look with great apprehension at the intervention of the nuclear powers in local wars fearing that they might lead to an outbreak of a world-wide nuclear conflict. Turning our attention to the world-wide problems of ecology, nutrition, population and resource depletion[75], we find further cause for anxiety at these other threats to world peace.

Mankind now stands at the crossroads of survival or extinction. We, as one world, must terminate conflicts

---

70) [名]後悔　71) [形]病気がまん延する　72) [名]憎しみ、恨み　73) trample upon~　~を踏みにじる　74) thermonuclear war 熱核戦争　75) [名]枯渇

which separate nation from nation and people from people. We must rid ourselves of nuclear weapons forever. The peoples of the world must come to realize that all men are members of a common human community. We must quicken our pace towards an everlasting world peace founded upon the concepts of human dignity and interdependence.

In the near future, the Mayor of Hiroshima will accompany the Mayor of Nagasaki to the United Nations to give testimony as living witnesses to the grim realities of the atomic bomb experience. They will propose before all the nations of the world that all the people of the world are potential survivors. The mayors of Hiroshima and Nagasaki are further resolved to request the General Assembly for an early realization of concrete measures to abolish nuclear weapons. Such measures are seen as being consistent with resolutions previously adopted by the General Assembly concerning the Prohibition of the Use of Nuclear Weapons[76], Non-Proliferation of Nuclear Weapons, and the Banning of Nuclear Weapon Tests[77].

Standing in front of the A-bomb sacrificed souls today, we hereby renew our pledge for peace and solemnly declare the above to the world at large.

*   *   *

76) Prohibition of the Use of Nuclear Weapons 核兵器使用禁止
77) Banning of Nuclear Weapon Tests 核実験停止

Peace Declaration (1975)

【A comment by the City of Hiroshima】
〈Detailed accounting of the reality of the A-bomb damage〉

On August 6, 1945, an atomic bomb exploded, without warning, high above the citizens of Hiroshima.

A searing heat flashed from the bomb, a cataclysmic[78] detonation[79] shook the earth, and in an instant Hiroshima City was levelled.

The toll of the dead and injured mounted, while in a pall[80] of dense black smoke an unearthly inferno became a reality.

Beneath the collapsed structures of buildings, in the midst of raging flames, people lay dying, desperately pleading for help. In the streets people collapsed and died; in the rivers bodies drifted, floating and sinking; and a ragged and bloody procession wandered blindly, seeking safety away from the mad and frantic streets, while voices begged 'water, water' as they weakened and neared death. Thirty years have elapsed, and all still linger in our minds today, penetrating our hearts with pain and regret.

And beyond this, countless survivors in their lives today cannot rid themselves for a day of agony and fear that radio-activity[81] has inflicted on them. Hiroshima testifies with her body and soul against this inhumanity.

Moved by the ordeal of suffering that has stemmed

78)［形］地殻が変動する、壊滅的な　79)［名］爆発　80)［名］覆って暗くするもの　※in a pall of dense black smoke 黒煙もうもうたる中で　81) radio-activity 放射能

from the atomic bomb, the citizens of Hiroshima have called for and sought peace for mankind, unceasingly and steadfastly pleading that the Hiroshima disaster never again be repeated.

And still in the world today we see nations and people everywhere perturbed[82] by the menace of nuclear weapons.

The countries possessing nuclear weapons have ignored the protest of Hiroshima and not only continue nuclear tests, but absorb themselves in developing these bombs. Following their lead, other countries are oriented towards arming themselves with nuclear weapons and thus intensify the proliferation of nuclear arms.

The world today is in an era of chaotic nuclear competition, at the threshold of a grave crisis that could lead to the annihilation of mankind, a reality that the citizens of Hiroshima absolutely cannot make light of.

Individual human beings must realize that we live on the same earth as respective members sharing a destined community, and so must stand out resolutely for the abolition of all nuclear weapons.

Facing this formidable situation, Hiroshima City has renewed her resolution to build a true world of peace by formally affiliating with Nagasaki, the city like Hiroshima suffered the horror of nuclear bombing. We wish that our concept of peace be in harmony with that of mankind in entirety.

On this day when we remember and mourn the souls

---

82) perturb［他動］不安にさせる、動揺させる

of those who were sacrificed, we hereby plead with all our strength to the people of the whole world that it is high time to abolish all nuclear weapons since they are threatening the extinction of the humanity we should be trying to protect.

CHAPTER 5

SETSUO YAMADA's[1]
PEACE DECLARATION
(1974–1967)

Peace Declaration (1974)

【Comments by the City of Hiroshima】
〈Prevention of nuclear proliferation; first concrete proposal to the United Nations〉

On the observance of the twenty-ninth anniversary of the atomic bomb devastation, and with the concurrent[2] grievous international climate of consecutive nuclear testings and proliferation of nuclear weapons, and in behalf of the citizens of Hiroshima I strongly remonstrate[3] and dissuade[4] the nuclear possessing nations of the United States of America, the Union of Soviet Socialist Republics, the People's Republic of China, France, Great Britain, and India to: "Promptly halt all nuclear testings and abrogate[5] what nuclear weapons are in any stockpile."

The United States and Soviet Russia in assuming leadership in the world politics seem to have as their new political and diplomatic strategy the intention to grant nuclear aids to the developing countries,

1) 山田節男（市長任期1967年5月〜1975年1月）　2) ［形］同意見の
3) remonstrate［他動］抗議する　4) dissuade［他動］思いとどまらせる
5) abrogate［他動］廃棄する

designated to expand their respective influences, thus encouraging nuclear proliferation.

At this high time in the trend for nuclear weapons to be compact a special warning must be given that a strong possibility is emerging for even the developing countries to have easy access to nuclear possession somewhat in terms of conventional weapons.

This signifies the easy usage of nuclear weapons in the limited wars, an awesome manifestation but an imminent reality.

Under the guise of nuclear equilibrium theory[6] or self-defense, the rapid nuclear proliferation is opening the path to suicidal ruin of total mankind. And the critical moment is approaching, here and now.

In order to decisively put a stop to the precarious headway[7] of nuclear proliferation, we will appeal to the United Nations to convene an emergent international conference for an early conclusion of a total nuclear ban agreement, including all nuclear possessing nations, and also to the Japanese government to urge for an early ratification of the non-nuclear proliferation treaty.

"Do not repeat Hiroshima." We hereby again ring and precaution these words to the nuclear powers as well as to the third world which is being oriented toward nuclear possession.

We must deeply recognize that all men can live together in one world sharing common destiny, and that each and all members must endeavor to create a

6) nuclear equilibrium theory 核均衡の理論　7) [名]進行

world community founded on world citizenship. This is the only right road to establish a long and lasting peace for the sake of all mankind.

Before these sacrificed souls, in behalf of the Hiroshima citizens, I hereby solemnly declare to the whole world that we will ever renew in very strong terms our vow to win peace on this invaluable earth.

*　　*　　*

Peace Declaration (1973)

【A comment by the City of Hiroshima】
〈Strong criticism of the nuclear powers〉

On this day of twenty-eight years ago, the atomic bomb devastated Hiroshima in one instant and took the lives of more than two hundred thousand citizens. The documentary photographs of the atomic bomb disaster recently released to the public after their return by the United States government have again made vivid the disastrous consequences of this event. The impact of these has resulted in a renewed intellectual and emotional realization of the hatred of war and desire for peace that form "the heart of Hiroshima."

As we observe Atomic Bomb Memorial Day today, we firmly appeal to all people in the world in these words: "Hiroshima should never by any means be repeated."

The Vietnam cease-fire agreement has at long last been concluded, and the normalization of diplomatic relation between Japan and the People's Republic of China has come into view. A thaw in the international climate seems to be beginning. Yet there is still no firm political guarantee that assures the termination of nuclear wars. France has ignored the strong protests of the entire world and carried through its nuclear testing in the South Pacific. The United States of America, the Union of Soviet Socialist Republics, and the People's Republic of China are still continuing nuclear testings. They all attempt to justify themselves for the sake of national security shielded by, what we call, national sovereignty[8], an excuse that is not merely anachronistic[9], but more importantly, a criminal act against all mankind.

So that nuclear weapons may be abolished promptly, and nuclear testing be ended immediately and completely, citizens everywhere in the world must find ways to bring their efforts into a strong united movement. Dedicated and sincere education for peace is the true source of world harmony. "The heart of Hiroshima" is passed on as a living legacy to the coming generations. And consistent with progress in peace education and peace research, we actively call upon the whole world for the creation of a new civilized community based upon human dignity.

Wars have their inception within the minds of men. When we directly observe the realities of today, namely,

8) [名]主権　9) [形]時代錯誤の

the environmental destruction sweeping all over the world, the pressure of population growth, the exhaustion of natural resources that quickly leads to critical shortages of food and other human necessities, and then we feel deep apprehension for the desolation that can be perceived in the human spirit, and for all the factors that potentially threaten peace in the world.

True peace in the world can only be assured by the establishment of world order governed by world law. In circumstances where mundialization[10] is inevitable[11], security and prosperity for the self-interest of any single nation is beneath consideration. We are now in an age of transition: the age of the nation state is behind us, and the age of the world state just ahead of us. The solidarity and co-operation of the entire world is the only road to betterment of conditions and, indeed, to survival. I cannot state this too strongly.

As we stand here in presence of the souls of the victims of the atomic bomb, we renew our vows of peace, and declare the above, in the name of the entire citizenry of Hiroshima, to all people in our nation and of the whole world.

* * *

Peace Declaration (1972)

【Comments by the City of Hiroshima】
〈First reference to the United Nations; problems

---

10)［名］世界化　11)［形］必然的な

besides war (environment, natural resources, etc.); first
use of the phrase "Spirit of Hiroshima"⟩

Today, as we observe the twenty-seventh anniversary
of the atomic bomb dropping, the day with all its
disastrous memories haunts our minds retracing
pang[12] and agony. Incessantly in search for an
unquestionable world peace through appeal for
abolition of nuclear weapons and renunciation of war,
the "Heart of Hiroshima" has served to revive the conscience of mankind and undoubtedly had functioned
as a deterrent against nuclear wars. However, being
possessed by the idea of balance of power, the great
nuclear powers have poured preposterous[13] sum of
wealth and knowledge into the armament and have
extensively proliferated the crisis of a nuclear war.

On viewing the recent international trend, namely,
the summit meetings held between the United States of
America and the People's Republic of China, between
the U.S.A. and the U.S.S.R., the East Treaty concluded
between West Germany and the Union of Soviet
Socialist Republics, and new move of governmental-
level negotiation for restoration of diplomatic relation
between Japan and the People's Republic of China; all
seems to denote[14] receptive auspices[15] of a thaw in the
cold war, at long last. Whereas on the Vietnam front,
the beholder[16] is obliged to avert his eyes from the
tormented scene of numberless women and children
performed by the magnitude scale of strategic bombing

---

12) [名]心の痛み　13) [形]途方もない、馬鹿げた　14) denote [他動]示す
15) [名]前兆　16) [名]見る人

and destruction. In the meantime, nuclear testings are forged ahead by the alleged nuclear powers utterly ignoring the sincere protest lodged by Hiroshima.

We, restate our strong appeal to expedite the termination of the Vietnam War and earnestly desire for an early realization of total ban on all nuclear weapons, without the least forgiveness on whatever nuclear testing, conducted by any nation whatsoever.

We, hereby affirm that the notion to believe nuclear armament could and would enhance one's own national security is nothing but mere delusion.

At the recent United Nations Conference on the Human Environment, the concept of human survival in the 1970s has been clarified, recognizing the destruction of natural environment, the population augmentation, and the multiple phases of crisis that mankind is confronted with; and whereby a declaration was pronounced for an urgent international consensus oriented towards a complete abolition of nuclear weapons. This event is in full accord with the very ideal of the Japanese Constitution on her renunciation of war, which directs to the road of peace.

It is high time that we call upon nations in the world to challenge the serious undertaking of education for peace and research for peace. In order to inherit this peaceful and livable earth on to the coming generation, we should reflect and realize that mankind partakes the same destiny existing on one earth, and by surpassing all ideological differences and binding intellectual and spiritual ties, we should create a new world order in which man neither has to kill nor be killed. This, we believe is the condition that will prevent another Hiroshima in the coming world.

In front of the victims, on this day of the Atomic Bomb anniversary, I hereby declare our renewed vow for peace, widely and strongly, to the entire world.

*   *   *

Peace Declaration (1971)

【A comment by the City of Hiroshima】
〈Necessity of education for peace〉

The general situation of the world is marked by a keen armament race frantically contested by enlisting the whole scientific and technological force, thereby developing a nuclear weaponry system of growing monstrosity[17] and diversification[18] that has aggravated the fear of the world to the last limit with its incredibly destructive power and radiation hazards. On the other hand, warlike actions in Vietnam are being repeated endlessly, exposing the inhabitants of the area to miserable death and hopeless suffering by tens of millions. As we stand now before the consecrated[19] souls of the victims of the atomic bombing, this state of affairs fills our hearts with profound grief, and we feel a strong urge to condemn it as wholly impermissible.

---

17) ［名］巨大化　18) ［名］多様化　19) consecrate［他動］捧げる

While all men are born free and equal in dignity and rights, war violates the fundamental human rights and as such is an inexcusable crime. All the more so is a modern war, inasmuch as it is clear that, if carried to the extreme, it would invite nuclear retaliations which would plunge mankind into the crisis of total annihilation.

The wound inflicted on Hiroshima by the atom bomb of twenty-six years ago today was of far-reaching nature: the human lives deprived by it reached a quarter-million, and the survivors exposed to its radiation still live under its constant threat to their life, while its fullest effects yet lie hidden from man's knowledge. The lesson of this terrible experience teaches that the nuclear weapons should be abolished and all wars totally renounced.

Thus we offer this proposition: Now is the time to formulate a well-defined concept on human existence; to fully realize the fact that we as inhabitants of the earth all share one and the same destiny; and, by setting up a new world structure founded on the awakened consciousness of world-citizenship, to build a human community free from all wars. This will entail upon[20] all nations of the world that they act upon the fundamental spirit in which the Japanese Constitution has renounced wars, and liquidate[21] their military sovereignty completely by transferring it to a world organization binding mankind in solidarity. As prerequisite[22] to this, we strongly demand immediate

---

20) entail upon~ ～を強いる　21) liquidate [他動] 解消する　22) [名] 必要条件

halting of all current wars on earth and speedy conclusion of an agreement banning the use of nuclear weapons. Furthermore, in order that the meaning of war and peace may be handed down infallibly[23] to the coming generations, education for peace should be promoted with vigour[24] and cogency[25] throughout the world. This should be the absolute way to avoid the recurrence of the tragedy of Hiroshima.

We appeal this to the world far and wide as we observe today the twenty-sixth anniversary of the destruction of Hiroshima by the atomic bombing and pay our homage to the fallen victims of the catastrophe.

*　　*　　*

Peace Declaration (1970)

When man's science glories in the achievements in the outer space, on earth the yet unmitigated[26] distrust among the nations is repeatedly engendering the crime of armed hostilities, such as is witnessed in the deplorable realities in Vietnam and the Middle East.

Hiroshima has attested to the eventual possibility of human extermination[27] from the earth if the nuclear weapons were to be unleashed for actual use. In face of Hiroshima's protest, however, the major powers of the world, ever engrossed in[28] the endless race of nuclear armament, are treading the path to man's self-destruction.

The first atomic bomb in man's history was dropped

---

23) [副] 絶対確実に 24) [名] 活力 25) [名] 説得力 26) [形] 和らげられな
い 27) [名] 絶滅 28) engross in~ ～に夢中になる

on Hiroshima twenty-five years ago today, when our city was reduced to utter ruins in a flash and the loss of precious human lives numbered more than two hundred thousand. Even now, the bomb survivors are constantly threatened by its potential menace to life. Such a dire catastrophe should under no circumstances be ever repeated.

Since that fatal day, our knowledge of the human disaster in Hiroshima has kept alive our call for the abolition of nuclear weapons and the renunciation of wars, which, favorably supported by the world-wide opinion, has contributed, to say the least of it, to prevent the use of nuclear weapons. This achievement inspires us to further consolidate our national aspiration for peace as well as to help implant the experience of Hiroshima deep in the hearts of all people of the world in order to advance our cause aimed at the total elimination of nuclear weapons and the realization of an everlasting peace of the world.

It is now high time that a citadel[29] for peace be built within the hearts of all men. Peace can no longer belong to a single nation alone. The world is one and mankind is of one inseparable body. Acting on the consciousness of all men being world-citizens, we should establish a world-wide order of peace ruled by a World Law founding itself on the spirit of universal interdependence of all human beings.

On this day that marks the twenty-fifth anniversary of the atomic bombing of Hiroshima, we strongly call

---

29) [名]とりで

out to the world with this appeal, as we solemnly pray for the repose of the departed souls of the victims.

*   *   *

Peace Declaration (1969)

Today we commemorate the anniversary of the atomic bombing over again.

On this day twenty-four years ago, Hiroshima was reduced to ashes in less than no time, and the human lives taken away counted more than two hundred thousand. The radioactivity, moreover, having penetrated deep into human bodies, continues to this day to menace the life of the survivors. With the lapse of time, however, the people of the world tend to forget the grievous ravages of the atomic bomb and even their sense of its dreadfulness[30] is being blunted[31].

The atomic and hydrogen bombs are weapons that bring not only mass destruction but also radioactivity, and it is crystal-clear that the earth, if covered all over by the proliferating radioactivity, would ultimately become uninhabitable for man. This not-withstanding, the major powers of the world are making desperate efforts to augment their nuclear armaments on the pretext of balance of power, inevitably spurring on humanity on its way to self-destruction.

Precisely in this context we see man's dream of landing on the moon come true. This most magnificent achievement of this century not merely adds glorious

---

30) [名]恐ろしさ　31) blunt[他動]鈍らせる

prestige to the experimenting nation alone, but it is the fruit of modern science and technology, and represents the triumph[32] of human intelligence. We should strive to make this triumph a turning point toward man's ideal of all living and letting live, in prosperity shared by all. Having brought himself to the threshold of the space age, man should make use of his extended horizon and elevated viewpoint to expunge his conventional ways of thinking and proceed to establish a completely new conception of the world.

The world is one and mankind is of one inseparable body. The time has fully come for us to formulate a clear concept and thought on human existence; to take due cognizance[33] of the fact that we as inhabitants of the earth all share one and the same destiny over and beyond the barriers of national sovereignties and the irreconcilabilities[34] between the diverse social systems; to set up a new world order founded on a world law that is based upon the professed concept of world-citizenship; and to build up a world community that should be free of all wars. To realize this would prove a citadel against any recurrence of 'Hiroshimas' on earth; it should indeed be the mission of all those who live in the shaping of contemporary history.

For this we strongly appeal to the whole world, on this occasion of congregating today to pray for the repose of the souls of the fallen victims of the atomic bomb.

---

32) [名]勝利　33) [名]認識　34) [名]和解できないこと

✳   ✳   ✳

Peace Declaration (1968)

【A comment by the City of Hiroshima】
〈Clear criticism of the policy of nuclear deterrence〉

Today we greet the returning anniversary of the atomic destruction of our city. On this day twenty-three years ago, Hiroshima was reduced to ashes in a moment and human lives were destroyed in countless numbers. Furthermore, the radioactive emanations which then penetrated deep into the human body present continued threats even now to the life of the survivors, filling their hearts with unspeakable apprehensions.

It is not simply that the nuclear bomb is a powerful weapon of mass destruction; obviously, its radioactive emissions diffused over the earth will eventually preclude[35] human habitation on it, a dreadful consequence which a large segment of the world population still remains unaware of.

Nuclear disarmament, though already on the agenda of international politics, does not necessarily promise a total abolition of nuclear arms; it may, on the contrary, seriously jeopardize the world by poising it on a balance of power, for to regard unclear weapons as an effective war deterrent[36] will only serve to spur the nuclear race, the ultimate end of which will be linked with the end of mankind.

---

35) preclude［他動］不可能にする、阻止する　36) war deterrent 戦争抑止力

The existing state of affairs demands that a retrospective reference be made constantly to the experience of Hiroshima. The misgivings that we felt at the time of the atomic bombing about the self-destruction of mankind should be brought back to mind anew, and our initial determination revived to make the voice of Hiroshima the voice of the world. This is a task devolved on the citizens of Hiroshima and a mission on the part of those awakened to the crisis of the century.

All weapons are forged by man, and all wars are waged by man; by no means should it be beyond man's power to triumph by his own hands over the abominable[37] arms and wars. It is high time for the nations of the world to make an express determination that all efforts spent on war-making be concentrated on the building of an ideal world where mankind may share in common prosperity. The world is one, and all the men are human brothers. Creation of a society governed by justice and a new world order should verily[38] be the task imposed on us as bearers of the glory of humanity.

We, the citizens of Hiroshima, ever since that fatal day, have set our hearts on the absolute banning of nuclear bombs and complete abolition of wars, and at no time have we desisted from[39] addressing this appeal to the world. As we pay homage to the victims of the atomic bomb today, we declare this once again with all the emphasis at command.

---

37) [形]忌まわしい　38) [副]本当に、確かに　39) desist from~ ～をやめる

*   *   *

Peace Declaration (1967)

August 6, 1945 has led us to the realization that on that day our world was forced to stand at the threshold of a new era. Life or death, annihilation or prosperity - these two and only two alternatives confront mankind today.

Indeed, the development of atomic energy crowned the twentieth century science with a brilliant victory, but the destiny of mankind has been made to test heavily on whether the great achievement of modern science will be employed for slaughter and destruction, or for human well-being and construction.

World peace, barely hinged on[40] the balances of power and of terror among the great powers, is as precarious as eggs piled one on top of another. Powerful armed forces pitted against one another in heavy reliance on nuclear weapons may easily explode into a war that may well drag mankind into its ultimate destruction.

For delivery from this anxiety and danger, there no longer remains any other way out but to set up, in the spirit of solidarity of mankind, a new world order where Law shall prevail, based upon tolerance and faith, conciliation and discipline. In place of battlefields, let there be prepared a seat for mutual understanding under dominance of true international amity and lofty world law; let there be established a world order for the

---

40) hinge on~ ～次第である

guarantee of mutual aid, cooperation and prosperous coexistence to all nations and peoples, banishing for good the tragedy of war from this earth. Only then will a permanent peace be created as fruit of the human wisdom, only then will a new era be ushered into[41] our world.

Eloignment[42] from sight begets oblivion; let us not forget the tragedy of Hiroshima that smote her like a bolt from the blue twenty-two years ago today, destroying more than two hundred thousand lives, and which even to this day threatens the life of many a surviving bomb-victim. Let it be remembered as an experience shared in common by all the world, and let our appeal ring out that all human intellect and power be concentrated so as to have any and all wars completely abandoned and nuclear weapons totally banned.

Thus we do proclaim far and wide to the entire world, as we today pay homage to the fallen victims of the Atom Bomb.

---

41) usher into~ ~を導く   42)［名］遠離

CHAPTER 6

SHINZO HAMAI's[1]
PEACE DECLARATION
(1966–1959)

Peace Declaration (1966)

The Sixth of August has come upon us again today.

Twenty-one years ago on this day, we, the people of Hiroshima, went through that dreadful catastrophe which led us to sense the advent of an age in which war would take on a radically different character.

A nuclear bomb is not merely a powerful weapon of destruction; its radioactivity, long infesting[2] both land and sea, becomes a menace to the life of living beings, and once used in large quantities, it would, as has been established, utterly pollute the atmosphere, eventually rendering the very earth unfit for human habitation. Furthermore, with technology capable of delivering rockets to the lunar surface, it would not take a difficult feat[3] to effect in an opponent country, simultaneously with the outbreak of hostilities, an utmost demolition of its cities and major installations, causing millions of casualties among its inhabitants at a single blow.

War in the nuclear age is no longer a means of self-defense, but nothing less than an act of suicide by mankind itself.

---

1) 濱井信三（市長任期1947年4月～1955年4月／1959年5月～1967年5月）
2) infest［他動］はびこる　3)［名］技能、芸当

It is most depressing, however, to see that even now one or two nations are forcing nuclear experiments in the atmosphere, aiming at the exploit of the diabolical[4] weapon, while in Vietnam, the Middle East, the Near East and elsewhere in the world, warlike conflicts are being pursued at grave risks.

We firmly believe that all nations and peoples should rise to the cause of human survival, laying aside all self-interests and past grievances, now that man has come to share his lot not so much with a particular nation as with the earth in its entity.

As we, on this anniversary of the atomic bombing, make homage to the memory of its victims, we once again declare the belief of the people of Hiroshima and appeal therewith to the whole world.

*   *   *

Peace Declaration (1965)

【Comments by the City of Hiroshima】
〈Banning of atomic and hydrogen bombs and the complete renunciation of all war; regret for the Vietnam War〉

The twentieth anniversary of the atomic bombing is here with us today.

We, who witnessed the catastrophic ravages of that atomic bomb, have been led to the realization that our

---

4) ［形］悪魔の

conventional view on wars must undergo a radical change. In the nuclear age, war has come to mean nothing less than an act inviting ruin upon mankind itself, without distinction of friend or foe, for an atom bomb is not merely a dreadfully destructive weapon of barbarous cruelty, but it has also become clear that its radioactivity, while undermining human bodies over a long period of time, will ultimately make the very earth uninhabitable for man.

It is this realization that has constantly urged us, the people of Hiroshima, to voice our strong appeal for the banning of atomic and hydrogen bombs and for the complete renunciation of all war.

During the past twenty years, however, not only have nuclear weapons undergone prodigious[5] development, both in quality as well as in quantity, but the countries possessing them have gradually grown in number, all contributing to increasingly confuse the situation. Truly alarming is the further fact that armed conflicts involving grave risks are being repeated in Vietnam and elsewhere in the world. In our apprehension, never before has humanity faced a crisis greater than that of today.

This viewpoint should require all nations and peoples to strive for the prevention of man's downfall by exerting their utmost efforts, to which all previous international entanglements[6] should give way in view of the gravity of the situation. This, we firmly believe, is the imperative need of the present moment.

---

5) [形]驚異的な   6) [名]もつれ、紛糾

Today we reiterate this appeal to the whole world as we once again propitiate the manes of those who perished in the atomic bombing.

*   *   *

Peace Declaration (1964)

August 6th is here with us again today.

Nineteen years ago today, the City of Hiroshima was suddenly reduced to cinders[7] and countless human lives were taken away; even to this day the radioactive contamination that penetrated deep into the bodies of the survivors on that day continues to endanger their lives.

Remembering the depths of these miseries, we, the people of Hiroshima, have at every opportunity made known our experience to all the world and repeatedly appealed for the abandonment of nuclear weapons and abolishment of all wars.

With great gratification we have greeted the partial test ban treaty[8] that came into existence last year, initiated by the three powers, the United States of America, Great Britain and the Soviet Union, and joined by many other nations. While it certainly marked a step forward toward our ultimate goal, as such it is by no means an assurance for a complete abandonment of nuclear weapons and our present world sees international skirmishes[9] going on persistently at various locations, charged with grave dangers.

---

7) [名]燃え殻、灰   8) partial test ban treaty   部分的核実験禁止条約
9) [名]小競り合い

It is our hope that people throughout the world take to heart afresh that a war in the nuclear age would be nothing less than a means of total annihilation nor only for the belligerent nations[10] alone, but also for the whole mankind and that they further lend their efforts at attaining a complete abolition of all wars.

As we pay homage today to those who fell in the atomic catastrophe, we once again proclaim this far and wide to all peoples of the world.

＊　　＊　　＊

Peace Declaration (1963)

【A comment by the City of Hiroshima】
〈Praise for the conclusion of the Partial Nuclear Test Ban Treaty〉

We are gathered today to observe the eighteenth anniversary of the atomic bombing of Hiroshima.

Looking hard at the dreadful scars inflicted by the atomic holocaust which we have barely survived, we have kept appealing to the people of the world for the past eighteen years that the tragedy of Hiroshima should never be allowed to repeat itself.

The faith which we have in the meantime unswervingly upheld in man's goodwill and wisdom brings us today great gratification in that at long last a pact for the partial banning of nuclear weapons has been concluded

---

10) belligerent nations　戦争当事国

among the United States, the United Kingdom and the Soviet Union.

It is true that the pact still leaves some fundamental problems unsettled; nevertheless, we attach great significance to it as having carried our earnest wish a step forward to its ultimate realization.

It should be highly desirable at this juncture[11] that even greater efforts at achieving a total abolition of nuclear weapons and a complete renunciation of wars be spent by all peoples and nations in full realization that a war in the nuclear age would be nothing less than a means leading to annihilation not only the warring powers, but also the whole mankind.

On this day of commemoration that we observe for the bomb victims with renewed remembrances, we once again put forth this appeal to all people of the world.

＊　　＊　　＊

Peace Declaration (1962)

【A comment by the City of Hiroshima】
〈Importance of conveying A-bomb experiences to posterity〉

Today, we observe the return of that day of sad memory.

Seventeen years ago today, Hiroshima, which was

11) at this juncture この局面で、この重大時に、この段階で

founded by the great work of our fathers through the history of four hundred years, was totally ruined in an instant, and a heavy toll of lives was taken without distinction of age or sex.

What had arisen in the mind of us who had witnessed the disaster was a limitless hatred against war and a firm commitment that we would never repeat such tragedy.

Since then, we have taken every opportunity to tell our experience to the world and appeal for the prohibition of the use of nuclear weapons and for the need of the renunciation of war.

However, the production and tests of nuclear weapons have never been ceased so far, and to the worse, their destructive capability has become greater than ever. Accordingly, the confrontation among the nations gets intensified, thus having the world thrown into an unprecedented danger.

It is high time that people must fully recognize that, in the nuclear age, no war can bring a victory to any country, and that once it happens, it means not only the end of countries concerned but also that of the world.

We eagerly hope that all the people and nation, based on the spirit of human solidarity, devote themselves with all their might to the prohibition of nuclear weapons and to the renunciation of war, by surmounting petty differences between one another and giving priority to the common cause of us.

Today, we here make this appeal to the whole world,

renewing our homage to the souls of those who perished in the atomic bombing.

*　　*　　*

Peace Declaration (1961)

Today we observe the sixteenth anniversary of the destruction of Hiroshima by the atomic bomb.

On this day, in 1945, Hiroshima was reduced to ruins within a fraction of a second[12], and countless numbers of people were deprived of their lives. Moreover, the scars of the bombing have not disappeared after the passage of sixteen years, but continue to undermine people's life.

The experience of those people of Hiroshima who survived the horrible destruction made them foresee the possibility of the eventual annihilation of the world, should once again the atomic energy be employed as weapon. That it was by no means an exaggerated[13] apprehension is being borne out by[14] the rapid advance which followed subsequently in the achievements of science and technology.

It should now be clearly seen that a nuclear war will be a war without any victor, but will only lead to the suicide of mankind.

The time is not too late; now is the time for all peoples and all nations of the world to refrain from clinging to their own selfish claims and spend their efforts toward abolishing nuclear weapons and renouncing wars

12) within(in) a fraction of a second 一瞬で、たちまち　13) [形]誇張された
14) be borne out by~ ～によって裏付けられる

completely.

Thus do we declare to the world at large in the name of the citizens of Hiroshima as we this day bow low before the Cenotaph and pray for the repose of the souls of our fallen fellow countrymen.

*   *   *

Peace Declaration (1960)

A decade and a half have passed since the atomic bomb was dropped on Hiroshima.

On that day the City of Hiroshima was laid waste in a moment and lives without number were taken away. The catastrophe, however, implanted deep in the minds of those who had barely survived it a strong aversion[15] to wars and a firm stand against any recurrence thereof. Since then it has been our constant and earnest endeavor to make this cause known at every occasion.

However, the recent striding advances in the research and manufacture of nuclear weapons and the mounting tension in the international situation are indications inviting great apprehension. Now is the time for people to fully realize that an atomic war guarantees no victory, but only means self-destruction to mankind.

Let all nations and states, in the spirit of human solidarity, submerge their minor differences for more vital common interests, prohibit all nuclear weapons, abolish wars completely and establish a new world order in which all may live and make live in prosperity.

---

15) [名]嫌悪

This, to our best belief, is a task of the greatest urgency incumbent upon humanity.

Again we declare this to the world today as we with renewed memories pay homage to the souls of those who departed from us in the atomic bombing.

＊　　＊　　＊

Peace Declaration (1959)

Today we observe the fourteenth anniversary of that memorable day.

A city having a population of over four hundred thousand was instantly laid waste by a single atomic bomb and more than two hundred thousand precious lives were taken away en masse[16]; furthermore, even now after the passage of over a decade, it continues to take toll among those exposed to that evil flash.

The one prayer of the people of Hiroshima, as has been repeatedly embodied in our appeals, has been this: may all nations and states, acting in the spirit of human solidarity, unite in upholding their common cause over all minor differences to achieve the elimination of all wars and the total abolition of nuclear weapons.

Our world now faces the danger of annihilation by nuclear weapons. It should be clearly realized that a war in the atomic age will be a war with no victors, leading only to self-destruction of mankind. It is our belief that the creation of new international relationship and order

---

16) en masse［副］ひとまとめにして、集団で

to make way for peaceful coexistence is the foremost task imposed upon humanity.

As we pay homage to the souls of the atomic bomb victims today, we once again make this appeal to the world, and on our part pledge our devotion to the achievement of our aims with renewed determination.

CHAPTER 7

TADAO WATANABE's[1]
PEACE DECLARATION
(1958–1955)

Peace Declaration (1958)

【A comment by the City of Hiroshima】
〈First explicit appeal for a ban on atomic and hydrogen bombs〉

Today, as we, the citizens of Hiroshima, greet the return of another Peace Day, fresh memories revive in our retrospection[2] and countless emotions surge within our hearts.

Great was the misery brought by the atomic bombing of thirteen years ago, a tragedy unparalleled[3] in the annals of mankind, and to this day it threatens the lives of our survivors, as they still fall prey to premature death[4].

In the face of such painful reality, our aspiration for peace has kept us striving for the building of the Peace City of Hiroshima, to be symbolical of man's permanent peace. Today, as we see around us the flourishing green and the streets beautifully lined up with houses and buildings, we humbly pay homage to the souls of our

---

1) 渡辺忠雄(市長任期1955年5月〜1959年5月)　2) [名]回顧、追想　3) [形]類のない　4) premature death 夭折、若死に

departed, and strengthen our faith in peace.

With the public opinion ever rising toward the banning of nuclear weapons, the unilateral resolution declaring the halting of nuclear test and the opening of the technical conference of the air inspection system now seem to throw a faint ray of hope on the future, but still it behooves us to make our words more audible to all ears for the creation of a stronger public opinion, to exert ourselves for the establishment of an international agreement on the complete outlawing of the manufacture and use of all nuclear weapons, and thereby to save humanity from the crisis of its extermination.

Thus with renewed determination, and speaking from our own experience, we, the citizens of Hiroshima, do make this appeal to the world.

* * *

Peace Declaration (1957)

Today, on the twelfth anniversary of the destruction of our city by the atomic bomb, we, the people of Hiroshima, are in a position to evaluate the significance of the disaster with greater calmness and precision.

The instantaneous[5] force of destruction exhibited by the atomic bomb in its terrific heat and blast was indeed unprecedented, reducing Hiroshima to ruins almost inconceivable[6]. But in the new Hiroshima born thereafter on the debris[7] out of the strenuous[8] efforts of her citizens, a dreadful fact has come to light that the

---

5) ［形］瞬時の　6) ［形］想像も及ばない　7) ［名］がれき　8) ［形］たゆまざる

bomb has left yet another invisible force of destruction still at work in the body of the survivors. We now know that radioactivity once absorbed in a human body will continue to gradually undermine it, transmitting its devastating effects genetically down to posterity. Cases of premature death occurring from year to year among our survivors are feared to be indicative of [9] the grievous evils that will in all probability[10] persist into distant future.

Our present world is already exposed to the same evils of radiation in varying degrees. The current tests of atomic and hydrogen bombs are undermining, slowly but steadily, the very existence of mankind by the formidable amounts of radiation they release into the atmosphere.

As we stand today before the Cenotaph symbolizing the costly sacrifice offered by those who perished in the disaster, and pray for the repose of their souls, we feel ourselves urged to point out that all efforts directed at the bringing about of peace by dint of power, upon which ultimately rests the justification of the possession and testing of nuclear weapons, are doomed to be a sheer illusion. We therefore make appeal to the whole world that a true path to peace be chosen at once, to safeguard mankind from the greatest of crises that have ever confronted it, and in doing so, we solemnly pledge ourselves to do what is in our power to help achieve this end.

---

9) be indicative of~ ～を示す   10) in all probability たぶん、十中八九

＊　　＊　　＊

Peace Declaration (1956)

【A comment by the City of Hiroshima】
〈First appearance of the words "Ban on atomic and hydrogen bombs"〉

Today, on the eleventh anniversary of the atomic bombing on Hiroshima, we bow our heads silently before this Cenotaph which is a memorial for a large number of atomic bomb victims. We sincerely pray for the repose of their souls, and we once again express to the world our ardent desire for the realization of eternal peace.

Ever since the dreadful experience we met on that fateful day, we have repeatedly called for "No more Hiroshimas," to the world. Now, in response to our voices, at long last, we have got much sympathy and encouragement. Strong support has gradually been expressed for the campaigns against atomic and hydrogen bombs. Action is also now gradually being taken to develop relief measures for atomic bomb survivors who previously would have died because of insufficient medical treatment for many years. This gives us new encouragement.

The release of nuclear power has given a promise of limitless affluence to the life of the human race, but at the same time the tremendous destructiveness of nuclear power menaces the existence of humanity.

To decide to abandon the path to self-destruction, and to take the way toward prosperity require an immense effort from those who recognize and seek after peace in a true sense. Until the day when this important decision is made, we express our commitment to continue to speak about what we have learned from our experience, and we pledge ourselves to build the foundations upon which world peace can be established.

*　　*　　*

Peace Declaration (1955)

【A comment by the City of Hiroshima】
〈First reference to the plight of survivors〉

Today, on the occasion of the tenth anniversary of the atomic bomb dropping, we mourn with solemnity for the souls of the dead victims, and renew our fervent desire for and commitment to world peace, which have been earnestly expressed to the world on the basis of our tragic experience.

Six thousands of those who are suffering from A-bomb aftereffects are not still entitled to receive a proper medical treatment and are struggling against a hard life. Furthermore, ninety-eight thousands of survivors are incessantly threatened by the anxiety that they might be contracted with the A-bomb disease. We point out with great emphasis that the A-bomb radiation which gradually affects human body bears a danger that could lead the sound human society to the way for ruin.

We are not trembling with a groundless and exaggerated apprehension only because we did experience the atomic bomb explosion. We cannot remain an idle spectator of the status quo that all rest of the world seems as if it neglected that holocaust as a happening that took place at a tiny spot on the earth. We look on it as our great duty to tell this truth to the whole world and convey our appeal of "Never have the tragedy of Hiroshima repeated," until the day when we see the advent of an everlasting world peace in a true sense.

CHAPTER 8

SHINZO HAMAI's PEACE DECLARATION
(1954–1947)

Peace Declaration (1954)

【A comment by the City of Hiroshima】
〈Shortest text to date (320 letters in Japanese)〉

Today we reach the ninth anniversary of the tragic explosion of the A-bomb.

The bomb dropped on that day not only instantly took the lives of more than 200,000 of our citizens, but left effects that still threaten the lives of survivors in Hiroshima.

Furthermore, a yet more formidable weapon, the hydrogen bomb, has now appeared on the earth. Consequently the future of human beings is threatened and they face the possibility of self-extinction.

Was there ever a more menacing threat than this in human history?

We, the citizens of Hiroshima, cannot remain idle spectators of our own tragedy. We warn human beings that this tragedy must never be repeated again. We make a strong appeal for the total abolition of war and for the proper control of nuclear energy throughout the world.

As we work for peace, we offer a tribute of devout prayer to the souls of the A-bomb victims with determination to the establishment of peace.

*　　*　　*

Peace Declaration (1953)

It is eight years now since that most tragic day.

The citizens of Hiroshima will vividly remember the atomic desert created by the A-bomb. It was unimaginably terrible. And the scars of the crime perpetrated by that single bomb still linger among us. They warn us of the terror of war. This all-important lesson teaches us that we must not use weapons against each other. We must not destroy ourselves.

It was the great achievement of science to develop atomic energy. But it has brought us to a crossroads: we can either turn toward destruction and annihilation or toward the common welfare of mankind.

On this occasion, the eighth anniversary of the atomic bombing, undertake to inform the world over and over again of this truth. We make a vow[1] to the souls of the A-bomb victims that we will renew our devoted efforts towards the establishment of world peace.

*　　*　　*

---

1) make a vow 誓う

Peace Declaration (1952)

No time passes in vain. For seven years now we have been conscious of the terrible scars inflicted on our minds by the atomic disaster. We can not but[2] shudder at the tragedy that human fallibility[3] can cause.

Yet we affirm our faith in human goodwill and generosity.

We believe that there will be found a way which may be accepted in common by the people of the world, not degrading human dignity, but giving a dignity to human existence.

We must light a torch of love in one person's mind, so that it may pass to two people, and when the torch is lit as a sacred flame in the minds of all people, the world will surely be united in a circle of moral consciousness.

We offer a sincere pledge before the souls of the victims of the A-bomb, that we reflect in simplicity on the past, that we recognize our duty, and that we will carry it into practice, as responsible individuals and citizens of Hiroshima.

*   *   *

Peace Declaration (1951)

【A comment by the City of Hiroshima】
〈Message from the Mayor instead of Peace Declaration〉

---

2) can not but~ 〜せずにはいられない   3) [名]誤りを免れられない性質

A Milepost Towards The Achievement Of Peace

On this day, six years ago, our city was reduced to ashes in one instant, and the precious lives of more than two hundred thousand of our citizens were lost. This indescribable war damage indicates to us the danger for mankind of war and teaches us strongly that we should not spare any effort to realize everlasting peace. We are firmly determined that, ever mindful of the deep implications of that experience, we will work with all possible efforts, with the future generation in mind, toward the realization of the goal of peace.

August 6, itself is the day on which we build a milepost on the broad way to the achievement of everlasting peace. Whenever we, the citizens of Hiroshima, greet the return of another August 6, we should remember the past. We should also, however, make a fresh determination to proceed step by step to the establishment of the great ideal of the future. Today, on the occasion of this ceremony, we pray for the repose of the souls of the victims of the atomic bomb and offer our renewed vow for peace. We, three hundred thousand citizens here together, firmly pledge ourselves to build Hiroshima into a City of Peace.

*　　*　　*

No Peace Declaration (1950)

【A comment by the City of Hiroshima】
〈Fourth Peace Festival canceled (no Peace Declaration)〉[4]

*　　*　　*

Peace Declaration (1949)

On this day, four years ago, our city was reduced to ashes in a fraction of a second, and hundreds of thousands of our citizens died. Such a tragedy makes clear the awful danger of mankind's total destruction. A peaceful world can only be built by concentrating all our efforts and striving on the goal of peace.

Learning from this disaster, it is our duty to the world to dedicate ourselves to the pursuit of peace, for that is the only way in which we can repay the victims of the A-bomb for the sacrifice of their lives.

We rejoice to have the support of the people of the world in this, and to see the growth of a movement to designate August 6th as "World Peace Day" and to mark Hiroshima as a "World Peace Center." We are delighted to see a movement to establish a world organization dedicated to the permanent abolition of war.

The Hiroshima Peace Memorial City Construction Law[5] has been passed by the Japanese Diet and comes into force today. Today is the fourth occasion on which

4) Due to the outbreak of Korean War　朝鮮戦争勃発のため　5) Hiroshima Peace Memorial City Construction Law 広島平和記念都市建設法

we, the citizens of Hiroshima, have remembered our dead. We earnestly pray that such a tragedy will never occur on the earth again. We sincerely pledge ourselves to the creation of world peace and the culture of mankind to strive for a bright new age and the peaceful use of atomic power.

From this day on[6] let us abhor war and its terror and guilt, and strive for true peace. Let us forever reject war and educate mankind in the ideals of peace.

On this day, the fourth anniversary of the bombing, we pledge ourselves to world peace.

*　　*　　*

Peace Declaration (1948)

On the morning of this very day, three years ago, the city of our forefathers instantly turned into a city of death and darkness. The precious lives of more than one hundred thousands of our fellow citizens were thrown away. Even now the terrible scene of that destruction remains imprinted on our memories.

This devastation, however, shows us what a war in the future could bring. It warns us of the danger of the annihilation of mankind by war. At the same time it convinces us that it is not impossible for man to establish world peace, if we employ the efforts and ingenuities[7] which have been devoted to warfare to peaceful purposes. Putting this lesson to practical use is the only way to give meaning to the sacrifice of those

6) from this day on 今日この日から　7) [名]創意

victims who are at rest beneath the earth, and must be the greatest contribution we can make to the welfare of all mankind.

We, the citizens of Hiroshima, hold this solemn Peace Memorial Service to convey this lesson to the whole world, and we pray in sincerity that there may never be another Hiroshima in any part of the world.

History is nothing but the development of freedom and man's humanity, and the process of realization of God's will. We should believe in God's will and history, and trust "the justice and faith of people who love peace from all nations," thus establishing a bright era, which shall bring eternal peace and a new human culture to this atomic age.

Let us attain true peace by eradicating the act of war and the threat and crime of war.

Let us renounce war forever and establish the idea of world peace on this earth.

On this historic occasion of the third anniversary of the atomic bombing, we vow to achieve this goal by appealing for peace to the whole world.

＊　＊　＊

Peace Declaration (1947)

【A comment by the City of Hiroshima】
〈First Peace Declaration delivered at the first Peace Festival〉

Today, on this second anniversary of the atomic bombing of Hiroshima, we, Hiroshima's citizens, renew our commitment to the establishment of peace by celebrating a Peace Festival at this site, and expressing our burning desire for peace.

The citizens of Hiroshima will never be able to forget August 6, 1945. On that morning, exactly two years ago today, the first atomic bomb to be unleashed on a city in the history of mankind fell on Hiroshima; it instantly reduced the city to ashes and claimed the precious lives of more than 100,000 of our fellow citizens. Hiroshima turned into a city of death and darkness. Yet as some slight consolation for this horror, the dropping of the atomic bomb became a factor in ending the war and calling a halt to the fighting. In this sense, mankind must remember that August 6 was a day that brought a chance for world peace. This is the reason why we are now commemorating that day by solemnly inaugurating[8] a festival of peace, despite the limitless sorrow in our minds. For only those who most bitterly experienced and came to know most completely the misery and the guilt of war can utterly reject war as the most terrible kind of human suffering, and ardently pursue peace.

This horrible weapon brought about a "Revolution of Thought," which has convinced us of the necessity and the value of eternal peace. That is to say, because of this atomic bomb, the people of the world have become aware that a global war in which atomic energy would be used would lead to the end of our civilization and

---

8) inaugurate[他動]開始する

extinction of mankind.

This revolution in thinking ought to be the basis for an absolute peace, and imply the birth of new life and a new world. We know that, when in a crisis discover a new truth and a new path from the crisis itself, by reflecting deeply and beginning afresh. If this is true, what we have to do at this moment is to strive with all our might towards peace, becoming forerunners of a new civilization.

Let us join to sweep away from this earth the horror of war, and to build a true peace.

Let us join in renouncing war eternally, and building a plan for world peace on this earth.

Here, under this peace tower, we thus make a declaration of peace.

EPILOGUE

The epilogue of the book comprises UN Secretary-General António Guterres' full speech at the Hiroshima Peace Memorial Ceremony on August 6, 2022, his first visit to the city.

Excellencies, brave *hibakusha*, young peace activists, ladies and gentlemen.

Thank you for the honour of inviting me today.

［本日はお招きいただき、感謝申し上げます。］

Hon-jitsu wa, omaneki itadaki, kan-sha moushiage masu.

Seventy-seven years ago, tens of thousands of people were killed in this city, in the blink of an eye.

Women, children and men were incinerated[1] in a hellish fire.

Buildings turned to dust.

Survivors were cursed with a radioactive legacy.

Polluted by cancer.

Stalked by health problems.

And marked by telltale[2] scars on their bodies — the stigma of surviving the most destructive attack in human history.

The unflinching testimonies of the *hibakusha* remind us of the fundamental folly of nuclear weapons.

Nuclear weapons are nonsense.

---

1) incinerate［他動］焼いて灰にする、焼却する　2) ［形］紛れもない、隠し通せない

Three-quarters of a century later, we must ask what we've learned from the mushroom cloud that swelled above this city in 1945.

Or from the Cold War and the terrifying near-misses that placed humanity within minutes of annihilation.

Or from the promising decades of arsenal reductions and widespread acceptance of the principles against the use, proliferation and testing of nuclear weapons.

Because a new arms race is picking up speed.

World leaders are enhancing stockpiles at a cost of hundreds of billions of dollars.

Almost 13,000 nuclear weapons are held in arsenals around the world.

And crises with grave nuclear undertones[3] are spreading fast — from the Middle East, to the Korean peninsula, to Russia's invasion of Ukraine.

It is totally unacceptable for states in possession of nuclear weapons to admit the possibility of nuclear war.

Humanity is playing with a loaded gun.

There are signs of hope.

In June, members of the Treaty on the Prohibition of Nuclear Weapons met for the first time to develop a roadmap towards a world free of these doomsday weapons.

And right now, the Tenth Review Conference of the Treaty on the Non-Proliferation of Nuclear

3) nuclear undertones 核の潜在的脅威

Weapons is taking place in New York.

Today, from this sacred space, I call on this Treaty's members to work urgently to eliminate the stockpiles that threaten our future.

To strengthen dialogue, diplomacy and negotiation.

And to support my disarmament agenda by eliminating these devices of destruction.

Countries with nuclear weapons must commit to the "no first use" of those weapons. They must also assure States who do not have nuclear weapons that they will not use — or threaten to use — nuclear weapons against them. And they must be transparent throughout.

We must keep the horrors of Hiroshima in view at all times, recognizing there is only one solution to the nuclear threat: not to have nuclear weapons at all.

Ladies and gentlemen,

At the height of the Cold War, schoolchildren learned to hide under desks.

But leaders cannot hide from their responsibilities.

My message to them is simple:

Take the nuclear option off the table — for good.

It's time to proliferate peace.

Heed the message of the *hibakusha*:

"No more Hiroshimas! No more Nagasakis!"

And to the young people here today: Finish the work that the *hibakusha* have begun.

The world must never forget what happened here.
The memory of those who died — and the legacy
of those who survived — will never be extinguished.

INDEX

234

帝京新書001

「平和宣言」を英語で読む
—ヒロシマの心—

2023年12月10日　初版第1刷発行

編　者　帝京大学出版会
発行者　岡田和幸
発　行　帝京大学出版会（株式会社 帝京サービス内）
　　　　〒173-0002　東京都板橋区稲荷台10-7
　　　　　　　　　　帝京大学 大学棟3号館
　　　　電話 03-3964-0121
発　売　星雲社（共同出版社・流通責任出版社）
　　　　〒112-0005　東京都文京区水道1-3-30
　　　　電話 03-3868-3275
　　　　FAX 03-3868-6588
企画・構成・編集　谷俊宏（帝京大学出版会）
校　正　菱山繁（株式会社 ランゲージアートラボ）
装　丁　三浦正已（精文堂印刷株式会社）
印刷・製本　精文堂印刷株式会社

©Teikyo University Press 2023　Printed in Japan
ISBN：978-4-434-33127-5
無断転載を禁じます。落丁・乱丁本はお取り換えします。

帝京新書創刊のことば

日本国憲法は「すべて国民は、個人として尊重される」（第十三条）とうたっています。帝京大学の教育理念である「自分流」は、この日本国憲法に連なっています。自分の生まれ持った個性を尊重し最大限に生かすというのが、私たちの定義する「自分流」です。個性の伸長は生得的な条件や家庭・社会の環境、国家的な制約や国際状況にもちろん左右されます。それでも〈知識と技術〉を習得することにより、個性の力は十分に発揮されることになるはずです。「帝京新書」は、個性の土台となる読者の〈知識と技術〉の習得について支援したいと願っています。

グローバル化が急激に進んだ二十一世紀は、単独の〈知識と技術〉では解決の難しい諸問題が山積しています。国連の持続可能な開発目標（SDGs）を挙げるまでもなく、気候変動から貧困、ジェンダー、平和に至るまで問題は深刻化かつ複雑化しています。だからこそ私たちは産学官連携や社会連携を国内外で推し進め、自らの教育・研究成果を通じて諸問題の解決に寄与したいと取り組んできました。「帝京新書」のシリーズ創刊もそうした連携の一つです。

帝京大学は二〇二六年に創立六十周年を迎えます。

創立以来、私たちは教育において「実学」「国際性」「開放性」の三つに重きを置いてきました。「実学」は実践を通して身につける論理的思考のことです。「国際性」は学習・体験を通した異文化理解のことです。そして「開放性」は〈知識と技術〉に対する幅広い学びを指します。このうちどれが欠けても「自分流」は成就しません。併せて、解決の難しい諸問題を追究することはできません。「帝京新書」にとってもこれら三つは揺るぎない礎です。

大学創立者で初代学長の冲永荘一は開校前に全国を回り、共に学び新しい大学を共に創造する学生・仲間を募りたいと訴えました。今、私たちもそれに倣い、共に読み共に考え共に創る読者・仲間を募りたいと思います。

二〇二三年十二月

帝京大学理事長・学長　冲永佳史